Managing the Metrology System

Third Edition

Also available from ASQ Quality Press:

The Uncertainty of Measurements: Physical and Chemical Metrology:
Impact and Analysis
S. K. Kimothi

Failure Mode and Effect Analysis: FMEA from Theory to
Execution, Second Edition
D. H. Stamatis

HALT, HASS, and HASA Explained: Accelerated Reliability Techniques
Harry W. McLean

Concepts for R&R Studies, Second Edition
Larry B. Barrentine

The Desk Reference of Statistical Quality Methods
Mark L. Crossley

The Certified Quality Engineer Handbook
Donald W. Benbow, Roger W. Berger, Ahmad K. Elshennawy,
and H. Fred Walker, editors

To request a complimentary catalog of ASQ Quality Press publications,
call (800) 248-1946, or visit our Web site at http://qualitypress.asq.org.

Managing the Metrology System

Third Edition

C. Robert Pennella

ASQ Quality Press
Milwaukee, Wisconsin

American Society for Quality, Quality Press, Milwaukee 53203
©1992, 1997, 2004 by ASQ
All rights reserved. Published 1992. Third Edition 2004.
Printed in the United States of America

12 11 10 09 08 07 06 05 04   5 4 3 2 1

Library of Congress Cataloging-in-Publication Data

Pennella, C. Robert.
  Managing the metrology system / C. Robert Pennella.—3rd ed.
    p. cm.
  Includes bibliographical references and index.
  ISBN 0-87389-606-8 (acid-free paper)
    1. Engineering inspection. 2. Mensuration. 3. Quality control. I. Title.

TS156.2.P46 2003
658.5'68—dc22   2003016816

ISBN 0-87389-606-8

Publisher: William A. Tony
Acquisitions Editor: Annemieke Hytinen
Project Editor: Paul O'Mara
Production Administrator: Barbara Mitrovic
Special Marketing Representative: Robin Barry

ASQ Mission: The American Society for Quality advances individual,
organizational, and community excellence worldwide through learning,
quality improvement, and knowledge exchange.

Attention Bookstores, Wholesalers, Schools, and Corporations: ASQ Quality
Press books, videotapes, audiotapes, and software are available at quantity
discounts with bulk purchases for business, educational, or instructional use.
For information, please contact ASQ Quality Press at 800-248-1946, or write to
ASQ Quality Press, P.O. Box 3005, Milwaukee, WI 53201-3005.

To place orders or to request a free copy of the ASQ Quality Press Publications
Catalog, including ASQ membership information, call 800-248-1946. Visit our
Web site at www.asq.org or http://qualitypress.asq.org.

 Printed on acid-free paper

Quality Press
600 N. Plankinton Avenue
Milwaukee, Wisconsin 53203
Call toll free 800-248-1946
Fax 414-272-1734
www.asq.org
http://qualitypress.asq.org
http://standardsgroup.asq.org
E-mail: authors@asq.org

To my wife Anita.
Thanks for the understanding, support, and love.

In memory of Pasquale J. Di Pillo, PhD,
fellow, colleague, educator, mentor, and advocate
of the American Society for Quality
1934–2003

Table of Contents

List of Figures and Tables

Preface

In a rapidly changing world, it sometimes seems that measurement and standards are a haven of objectivity amidst the chaos of subjective opinion. Yet the standard that surrounds the subject of calibration as it affects quality often leaves suppliers thumbing through pages of jargon and lost in confusion. After a career in the field of quality, one lesson stands out: people will address quality issues when they have a clear picture of the actions and systems required to run a first-class quality and measurement operation. Conversely, when terminology and procedures are nebulous, energy that should be spent on implementation is lost on research, confusion, and frustration.

Chapter 1 addresses the needs of suppliers and their technical staffs by providing a step-by-step system for establishing, maintaining, and documenting an effective calibration system. The book clarifies the critical relationship of calibration to total quality management (TQM) and identifies both the mistakes that suppliers can find by measuring properly and the mistakes, or errors of omission, that are often overlooked until a crisis makes these errors all too obvious. Chapter 1 also describes the state-of-the-art techniques for planning and managing calibration systems as part of a cost-effective quality program.

The "how to" of setting up and auditing an effective calibration system appears in chapters 2 and 3. Readers will find a step-by-step system with examples and sample documents that can be quickly adapted to the specific requirements of their work settings. This chapter connects its recommendations to the American National Standards Institute (ANSI), the International Organization for Standardization (ISO), and the American Society for Quality (ASQ) Q9000 series standards. This chapter will help the reader who is making a transition from the U.S. government–published standard known as the MIL-STD-45662A, *Calibration System Requirements*. This chapter will also enhance the reader's efforts to become ISO certified or to adopt ISO standards. Since 1987 when ISO introduced quality standards in concert with ANSI and ASQ, businesses have been able to save money and improve results by achieving ISO supplier certification and registration. The reader will find that the application of the information in chapters 2 and 3 will contribute to those cost savings by reducing redundant effort and by capitalizing on proper preparation to support current or future ISO efforts.

Chapters 6 and 7 will assist the calibration professional in documenting capabilities and working procedures more effectively. The reader will be able to adapt the sample quality system manual in chapter 6 for use in documenting and clarifying calibration procedures. Chapter 7 helps the metrology professional adapt better methods to communicate the advantage of management's investment in the right human and technological resources to support an effective metrology program. Chapter 7 also demonstrates ways that correct calibration decisions can positively affect the bottom line.

ANSI/ISO/ASQ Q9001 and Q9002 do not specifically require the maintenance and use of quality cost data as a management element of a quality system program. However, chapter 7 "Costs Associated with Metrology Systems Management" will help those suppliers that elect to tailor their quality system manuals to accommodate cost of metrology data collection.

Chapter 8 "Self-Assessment of Metrology Systems" reinforces the information contained in this book. Additionally, the questions and answers will help the reader to apply calibration requirements contained in the ISO 10012-1 standard.

In summary, this book will help quality technicians and other supplier and customer personnel to readily recognize and establish a quality program with an emphasis on practical application. The integration of calibration into the scheme of a total quality system will help ensure not only the integrity of the total system but also contribute to the strength of the company's reputation, good will, and profitability.

This book is a labor that reflects the help and support of many people. The layout for the book's graphics was done by the skilled hands of Joan Wyndrum. I owe an ongoing debt of appreciation to Rosemary F. Garvey, the president of Blanchette Tool and Gage Manufacturing Company. Her willingness and ability to share her knowledge of the practical application of quality systems serves the profession well and has helped me greatly over the years. Editing and formatting help was provided by my colleague, Donna I. Mugavero, a gifted problem solver and a clear thinker. I also want to thank Jeanne K. Derbyshire, a trusted friend and colleague, for sharing her knowledge and experience regarding the role that metrology plays in the production of medical devices.

I am most grateful for the inspiration, sage critique, and guidance provided by Dr. Michael A. Pennella, who is not only an able writer but also a great son. Finally, I acknowledge my colleagues and friends in ASQ, notably Frank Corcoran, Fred DeNude, and the members of the ASQ North Jersey Section executive board for their commitment to a strong profession.

C. Robert Pennella
June, 2003

1
Overview

The proper application of a calibration system is one of the most important areas in which quality assurance (QA) personnel can positively affect the low quality and high costs associated with poorly manufactured products. Conversely, when a calibration system is ignored or improperly implemented, suppliers of goods and services can encounter a tarnished reputation at best and, potentially, financial disaster.

A properly implemented calibration system is the foundation of the inspection systems and quality programs that support the TQM strategy for the following reasons:

- Measurement confidence can be achieved only through the use of instruments of known accuracy.

- The accuracy requirements of measuring and test equipment (M&TE) are imperative to the corrective-action process aimed at the causes of nonconforming products.

- Process capability techniques cannot be used to full advantage unless M&TE and related measurements are reliable from the start.

PROJECT SIXTY

In the early 1960s, the U.S. government conducted a study titled *Project Sixty* to evaluate the feasibility of relying on the *inspection system concept* to determine the adequacy of supplies and services prior to their submission for acceptance by the supplier or the customer's QA representative. The objective of this concept was to ensure adequate quality throughout all areas of contract performance: planning, work instruction, fabrication, assembly, inspection, testing, storage, and shipping.

Project Sixty was put into service in 1965 with the support of Secretary of Defense Robert McNamara. Both the government and the private sector recognized that it was not only more economical but also more effective to establish and maintain an acceptable quality control system than to rely on end-item inspection to control product quality. The Project Sixty concept initially focused on defect detection but later relied on defect-prevention processes through the application of TQM principles based on the work of Dr. W. Edwards Deming and others.

The transition to preventive strategies was brought about by several factors. It was evident that no production or inspection system could be perfect and that not even 100 percent inspection of every item, as prevalent in the past, could preclude the acceptance of some defective supplies. Also, since the number of QA personnel that could be placed in a supplier's plant was small in comparison to the number of production personnel, the task of end-item inspection proved to be monumental.

Hence, today heavy reliance is necessarily placed on continuous process improvement, the hallmark of TQM. M&TE of known accuracy plays an important role in verifying the adequacy of relevant processes that lead to quality products and services.

EVALUATION PROCESS

To maximize the effectiveness of a supplier's inspection system or quality program, as well as support the objectives of TQM, all aspects of the metrology program must be carefully and continuously evaluated. If continuous improvement of the calibration policies and procedures is to be achieved, this evaluation process requires careful attention to those policies and procedures that lead to improved products and services.

Three decision-making factors affect the successful application of calibration policies and procedures. The evaluation process should be timely, unbiased, and all-inclusive. Each must be carefully considered and included in management planning:

1. *Timely.* The timely review of contract quality and product design requirements will:

- Eliminate any oversights that might lead to the production of nonconforming products

- Establish processes that lead to continuous product or service improvements

- Eliminate the presence of potential errors of omission

- Address the delivery constraints of the customer

- Reinforce the quality expectations of the customer

2. *Unbiased.* To maximize the quality effort and to ensure that the objectives of TQM are met, management must ensure that unbiased decisions are made regarding the policies and procedures and product-design requirements that lead to the calibration processes.

Decisions influenced by bias prevail when personnel fail to adhere to established processes. When policies and procedures are acceptable from the outset and are applied without undue subjectivity, the objectives of good quality will be met. However, when attention to details goes astray, good quality will also go astray. Sustained attention to established standards will greatly reduce biased conditions as well as reduce errors of omission.

Data used to evaluate the adequacy of process capabilities will be biased when the information represents an opinion of an individual rather than representing the intent of established written instructions. For example, the data will be biased if:

- The calibration technician calibrates M&TE under ambient conditions rather than under environmental conditions established by written instructions.

- The calibration technician arbitrarily decides to extend established calibration intervals, even though the calibration history indicates that this course of action is not justified.

- The calibration technician arbitrarily modifies calibration procedures without justification when calibrating M&TE rather than following the instructions furnished in specific documented calibration procedures.

- Human errors occur. Humans affect the application of a metrology system not only by what they do but also by what they do not do. The sources of human errors are threefold:

  - Inaccurate instruments

  – Inadequate description of calibration system

  – Errors of omission

3. *All-inclusive.* When management policy and procedures ensure that timely, unbiased, and comprehensive decisions are being made, success for the quality system shifts to the instruments used for measuring.

The accuracy requirements of M&TE play an important role in the accumulation of meaningful data. However, the calibration data that are generated are only as good as the reliability of the measuring equipment. Therefore, when measurements are made with measuring equipment of unknown accuracy, the quality of the data that is generated deteriorates. The critical role of instrument accuracy is covered under the following topics:

- The adequacy of measurement standards (MSs) and M&TE

- The importance of higher-level accuracy ratios between the MS and M&TE

- The method of selecting the best MS and M&TE for desired calibrations

- The impact that out-of-tolerance conditions have on instrument accuracy

- The traceability of M&TE to measurement standards of known accuracy

CALIBRATION SYSTEM DESCRIPTION

The objective of this book is to provide a step-by-step procedure for designing and implementing an effective and efficient metrology system that supports TQM by calibrating M&TE and using MSs of known accuracy. The step-by-step description of a calibration system in chapter 2 is intended to guide you through the establishment and maintenance of a calibration system. Chapter 3 "Metrology Audits," supports this discussion. Two case studies are also provided to demonstrate practical application of the calibration system. The case study in chapter 4 describes actions taken by a supplier with unknown calibration system capabilities. The case study in chapter 6 provides a generic example of a supplier's calibration system that can be used as an example for the development of calibration system documentation. The ANSI/ISO/Q9001 and Q9002 quality system standards do not specifically require the maintenance and use of quality cost data, yet many suppliers are concerned with these costs as a measure of their effectiveness. The ability of those involved with calibration to reduce cost while improving quality is addressed in chapter 7.

The type of calibration system that a supplier must put into effect depends on the complexity of the product design, contract quality requirements, and customer expectations. There are, however, some generic requirements that a supplier should be aware of from the outset of planning the calibration system.

CATEGORIES OF CONTRACT QUALITY REQUIREMENTS

Contract quality requirements fall into three general categories, depending on the extent of QA needed.[1] Knowing the differences between those categories plays an important part in establishing a calibration system that will be acceptable to both customer and supplier. The categories are:

Category 1. Under Category 1, responsibility for inspection is placed solely on the supplier wherein there is no requirement for participation in the QA process at the supplier's plant by the customer. This category normally applies to common, noncomplex items.

Category 2. Category 2 is known as standard inspection requirements. This category requires the supplier to have an inspection system that is acceptable to the customer. It neither specifies a requirement for the application of a specific inspection system nor a calibration standard. Normally, the selected inspection system and related calibration system requirement are determined by the supplier. This category applies to noncomplex, noncritical items.

Category 3. Category 3, which we will be dealing with in this book, is known as higher-level contract quality requirements. The detailed information that is required for the application of Category 3 contract quality requirements, which involve complex, critical items, is contained in chapter 2, "Calibration System Description." Where it is in the customer's interest that higher-level contract quality requirements be maintained, the contract shall require the prime contractor or its delegated subcontractor to comply with ANSI/ISO/ASQ Q9001-2000, *Quality Management Standards—Requirements,* or ISO 13485:2003, *Quality Management Systems—Medical Devices—System Requirements for Regulatory Requirements.* When higher-level contract quality requirements apply, the contract or purchase order shall require the supplier to comply with a calibration system that is normally referenced in the quality program or inspection system standard. In some instances, the calibration system requirement may be referenced separate from the quality program or inspection system standard. This action is taken by the purchaser when other than higher-level contract quality requirements are specified.

Many of the calibration system standards that were introduced to the public by the Department of Defense over the past five decades are now being replaced by standards published by ANSI, ASQ, ISO, the International Electrotechnical Commission (IEC), and the National Conference of Standards Laboratories (NCSL). A representative sample of these standards include:

- ANSI/ASQC M1-1996, *American National Standard for Calibration Systems*

- ANSI/ISO 17025-1999, *General Requirements for the Competence of Testing and Calibration Laboratories*

- ANSI/NCSL Z540-1-1994, *Calibration Laboratories and Measuring and Test Equipment—General Requirements*

- ISO 10012:2003, *Measurement management systems— Requirements for measurement processes and measuring equipment*

- ISO 13485:2003, *Quality Management Systems— Medical Devices—System Requirements for Regulatory Purposes*

Each supplier functions individually, and consequently the calibration system of each supplier might differ in specific method. Each standard presents certain basic functional concepts of a calibration system to ensure that M&TE is sufficiently accurate to ensure supply or service conformance to contractual requirements. For example, calibration requirements that involve Category 1 (common, noncomplex) and Category 2 (noncomplex, noncritical) items will not require an elaborate calibration system because of the loose tolerances of the items offered to the customer. The supplier will require lower accuracy levels of measuring equipment for these items. In addition, intervals of calibration for Category 1 and Category 2 items will be less frequent than those required for Category 3 (complex, critical) items, and the policies and procedures for Category 1 and 2 items are minimal in comparison to those for Category 3 items.

Category 3 items involve all of the elements of a calibration system. These types of items have tighter product tolerances, calibration intervals that are more frequent than Category 1 and 2 items, and policies and procedures that are more elaborate.

THE IMPORTANCE OF ESTABLISHING A CONSISTENT CALIBRATION SYSTEM

To ensure uniformity of understanding and to ensure continuity of satisfactory operations when personnel changes occur, all proposed or existing calibration procedures should be documented. Without written guides, policy and procedural questions are bound to arise and variations in practice that occur will result in confusion and uncertainty. Having a documented calibration system in place in the early stages of contract and technical review provides the supplier and those responsible for calibration with significant advantages. The supplier as well as the customer's QA representatives can complete their assigned functions by understanding and agreeing on the type of calibration required. The chapters that follow describe the steps that a supplier should take to establish a system for consistent calibrations.

A consistent calibration system does more than prescribe what is to be done to produce a quality product the right way every time. A consistent calibration system also prevents the unseen errors that manifest themselves in what is often unwritten in contracts and job descriptions and that often occur when someone overlooks something. These are the errors of omission.

Calibration system standards, like most other specifications, have inherent subjective characteristics. Standards specify *what* controls are to be implemented. It is the user's responsibility to define *how* the standard applies to products and services as well as *how* the requirements will be implemented. Therefore, a supplier must not fall into the trap of performing a cursory review of the contract quality requirements and product design requirements. Experience has shown that when this course of action is taken, errors of omission usually follow.

When potential errors of omission are prevalent, the adequacy of a calibration system will become suspect, staff will be questioned about the application of that system, and quality costs will be augmented. Errors of omission become evident when necessary procedures or work instructions are left undone or when established processes or work instructions are not implemented.

Errors of omission are minimized when a quality program, a TQM master plan, and an associated calibration system receive the support and commitment of management. This support is essential if:

• *The objectives of a calibration system are to be achieved.* The objectives of calibration systems management are maximized only when contract quality requirements are clearly defined between the purchaser and the purchaser's advisors. This is imperative for meeting the supplier's needs and interests as well as meeting the customer's needs and expectations. Having a clearly defined contract and associated technical documents is also imperative for management and operations personnel who hope to produce a product or service in accordance with contract quality requirements using inspection, measuring, and test equipment of known accuracy.

• *The quality expectations of the customer are to be satisfied.* Satisfaction of customer expectations is achieved when contract quality requirements are free from errors, ambiguity, and omissions and when specified requirements are clearly defined in a supplier's quality plan.

• *Reduced quality costs are to be achieved.* When technical requirements are clearly defined, suppliers of products and services will be able to meet contract requirements correctly the first time. They will also be in a favorable position to implement policy, procedures, and processes that are cost-effective.

The following are pertinent topics (quality elements) as well as potential omission factors that pertain to a calibration system and the impact that they have on the objectives of good quality when they are left undone or not implemented:

1. Planning process

    • Omission factors:

        – Prompt review of contract quality requirements

        – Identification of inspection and testing requirements

        – Required resources

    • Impact: The failure to review, identify, and summarize contract quality and product design requirements, the failure to ensure a clear understanding of technical requirements, and the failure to consider personnel, equipment, and facility requirements might jeopardize contract performance and delivery schedules and lead to unnecessary quality costs.

2. Organizational structure

    • Omission factors:

        – Authority

        – Responsibility

- Impact: The failure to establish responsibilities and authority might undermine the objectives of good management as well as employee morale. It might also compromise the QA expectations of the customer.

3. Contract administration

  - Omission factors:

    - Availability of pertinent technical data package

    - Supplementary contract quality requirements

    - Specifications

    - Drawings

  - Impact: The contract administrator must ensure that the complete technical data are made available to engineering, production, and QA personnel for their planning and implementation. The failure to provide a timely review of drawings, specifications, and other contract quality requirements might lead to:

    - Vague or ambiguous language or unsettled differences of opinion between the supplier and the customer prior to the start of production

    - Noncompliance with all contract quality requirements

    - Operations that are not cost-effective

    - Missed deliveries

4. Detailed contract and purchase order requirements

  - Omission factors:

    - Review

    - Summarize

    - Document

    - Implement

  - Impact: The failure of the QC manager or a designated representative to perform an in-depth review of specified requirements might result in:

    - Noncompliance with all specified requirements

– Customer complaints

– Delay in delivery schedules

– Unnecessary added costs

– Possible loss of repeat business

5. Policy procedures

   • Omission factor:

     – All of the applicable elements required in a calibration system

   • Impact: The preparation of policy procedures is required to support calibration processes. The absence of documented procedures will impede the substantiation of product quality and deter the objectives of process capability studies.

6. Product or service verification stations

   • Omission factor:

     – In-house and off-site product and calibration verification stations

   • Impact: The failure to identify inspection stations will impede the planning processes for the type and amount of calibration, inspection, and testing activity that will be required at the respective station.

7. Control of purchases

   • Omission factors:

     – Supplier capability

     – Supplier performance

     – Audits

     – Feedback data

   • Impact: When a proposed supplier's capabilities are unknown, the contractor should evaluate the supplier's qualifications prior to issuing a purchase order. A supplier with proven capabilities must substantiate its capabilities by furnishing ongoing objective evidence regarding QA operations. When controls are not established and implemented, there will be no assurance that required QA capabilities are adequately maintained.

8. Control of M&TE and MSs

   - Omission factors:

     - Adequacy and availability of M&TE and MSs

     - Policy procedures

     - System maintenance

     - Control of customer-furnished M&TE

     - Control of company-designed M&TE

     - Support to the purchasing manager

     - Calibration intervals

     - Traceability of M&TE and MSs

     - Calibration status

     - Calibration audits

   - Impact: The absence of some or all of the elements that comprise a written calibration system will lead to conditions that adversely affect the establishment, maintenance, and control of product quality and production capabilities. The accuracies of M&TE and MSs must be verified with higher-level standards if the integrity of the production processes is to be maintained. If the calibration system is to be cost-effective, it must include satisfactory provisions for maintaining M&TE and MSs that are used in-house as well as by subcontractors. The calibration system must also establish a procedure early in the process that will identify significant out-of-tolerance conditions.

9. Corrective action

   - Omission factors:

     - Correction of assignable causes

     - Adequacy of corrective action

     - Correction of unfavorable trends

     - Follow-up action regarding the adequacy of corrective action

   - Impact: The calibration system must provide for early detection and correction of reported out-of-tolerance conditions. Failure to take immediate corrective action might lead to additional staff hours and added cost.

10. Records

- Omission factors:

  - Accuracy

  - Completeness

  - Reliability

  - Nature of observation

  - Number of observations

  - Type and number of deficiencies

  - Corrective action taken

  - Monitoring of recorded information

  - Analysis of records

- Impact: The absence of objective records will impede the objectives of good management. The collection, review, and analysis of objective records are necessary to measure the effectiveness of a supplier's calibration system as well as to indicate the supplier's calibration capabilities.

11. Storage and handling

- Omission factors:

  - Handling practices

  - Packaging and transportation

  - Storage of M&TE and MSs

- Impact: Without a procedure to control the storage, handling, and transportation of M&TE and MSs, the user might doubt the accuracy of the measuring equipment as well as the instruments' control and maintenance.

RESPONSIBILITIES

A supplier's responsibility does not end with in-plant metrology actions. A supplier is also responsible for the accuracy of all measurements and calibration functions performed by outside sources, such as an independent laboratory or a subcontractor's plant. This need not result in complete uniformity or standardization of calibration policies or procedures between the contractor and subcontractor. However, the controls placed on the subcontractor should satisfy the requirements established by the procurement document. It is important to note that most functions of the calibration system are usually performed by the prime contractor. Therefore, the purchase agreement between the customer and supplier should focus only on those services that the prime contractor has elected to be performed by an outside source.

The responsibility for managing the metrology system is usually divided among the:

- QC manager

- Quality engineer

- Metrology manager

- Calibration technician

Some small companies cannot afford the expense associated with a full staff of managers. Under these conditions, all or most of the responsibilities are shared by the QC manager and the calibration technician.

Other companies utilize the full services of an independent calibration laboratory. Some companies might use an independent calibration laboratory to perform just a portion of the functions of the established calibration system, such as calibrating measurement standards or repairing some instruments.

Do not overlook the fact that the prime contractor is responsible for the quality functions performed by subcontractors. It is important, therefore, to ensure a clear understanding between the prime contractor and the subcontractor regarding calibration requirements imposed on the subcontractor. This clarity is usually stated in the purchase agreement and, when necessary, during a post-award conference between the prime contractor and subcontractor.

PLANNING FOR THE APPLICATION OF A CALIBRATION SYSTEM

The questions to consider during the planning process are threefold:

1. *What are the tightest product tolerances allowed for products and services offered?* The satisfactory identification and control of the tightest product tolerance will provide positive indications that other products with looser tolerances will be adequately controlled.

2. *What kind of calibration equipment is needed to check the product and M&TE?* Due consideration should be given to the accuracy level of the

M&TE and MSs that are required to check the product. A high accuracy ratio between the comparator and the item being checked will reduce potential measurement error.

3. *Will there be a need to solicit the services of an independent calibration laboratory to perform all or part of the calibration processes?* If the answer is yes, and if the suggested source is one with unknown calibration capabilities, the supplier must evaluate the capabilities of those potential outside sources prior to issuing a purchase order for required services.

DOCUMENTATION

Documentation is another important function of the calibration process. Without it, the selection of the required MS and M&TE might be compromised. Timely documentation of calibration requirements, when coordinated with inspection and testing requirements, will preclude the inadvertent omission of contract quality requirements and, at the same time, enhance the quality expectations of the customer.

MANAGEMENT SUPPORT

All of the topics that we will cover in this book will not work unless the supplier specifies its position regarding the importance of measuring equipment of known accuracy. An example here is useful. Not too long ago, a study was made on comparable M&TE between two companies. One company had established and maintained a documented calibration system, while the other company elected to recalibrate its equipment only when it was found to be unreliable. The results of this study conclusively showed that the cost per unit to calibrate only when M&TE was found to be unreliable was much greater than the cost of maintaining a documented calibration system through proper training and management. Hence, proper planning supported by documented policies and procedures rather than a crisis-only reaction will produce a calibration operation that excels and a business that is profitable.

ENDNOTE

1. U.S. Department of Defense, General Services Administration, and National Aeronautics and Space Administration, *Federal Acquisition Regulation*, part 46, clause 46.202 (1995).

2

Calibration System Description

Systems consist of elements working together to create an effective and efficient whole. Systems can consist of procedures, departments, manual and automated processes, or other elements that can be isolated and analyzed independently or in relation to other elements. Accordingly, a calibration system consists of several elements that, when understood, can produce dividends for a contractor and its customers.

Calibration systems meet two objectives:

1. Providing the customer with an indication of a supplier's calibration capabilities

2. Reducing quality costs through the early detection of nonconforming products and processes by the use of measuring equipment with known accuracy

The basic elements of a calibration system include:

- Responsibilities

- Planning process

- Environmental controls

- Intervals of calibration

- Calibration procedures

- Adequacy of MSs, inspection equipment, and M&TE

- Out-of-tolerance conditions

- Calibration sources

- Application of records

- Calibration status

- Control of subcontractor calibration

- Storage and handling

- Maintenance of policies and procedures

Several standards exist that set requirements for the establishment, implementation, and continuous control of the accuracy of inspection equipment and M&TE. These standards specify criteria that, when met, will be compatible to both the customer and supplier. Examples of such standards include:

1. ANSI/ASQC M1-1987, *American National Standard for Calibration Systems.* This standard specifies general requirements for the quality of calibration in accordance with established practices or objective QC techniques. This standard delineates the requirements for systems to calibrate measuring instruments to specified accuracies; it is intended to cover only the operations engaged in the calibration of instruments.[1]

2. ANSI/ISO 17025-1999, *General Requirements for the Competence of Testing and Calibration Laboratories.* This international standard specifies the general requirements for the competence to carry out calibration and other tasks, including sampling. It covers testing and calibration performed using standard methods, nonstandard methods, and laboratory-developed methods.[2] This standard is applicable to all organizations performing tests and calibrations, including first-, second-, and third-party laboratories where testing and/or calibration forms a part of inspection and product certification.[3]

3. ANSI/NCSL Z540-1-1994, *Calibration Laboratories and Measuring and Test Equipment—General Requirements.* Part I of this standard sets out the general requirements in accordance with which a calibration laboratory must demonstrate that it operates if it is to be recognized as competent to carry out specific calibrations. Part I applies to calibration laboratories' development and implementation of quality systems.[4]

Part II of this standard sets out the QA requirements for a supplier's system to control the accuracy of the M&TE used to ensure that supplies and services comply with prescribed requirements.[5] The role of the purchaser in monitoring a supplier's compliance with requirements of this standard may be fulfilled by a third party, such as an accredited or certification body.[6]

4. ISO 10012-1:1992, *Quality Assurance Requirements for Measuring Equipment—Part 1: Metrological Confirmation System for Measuring Equipment.* This part of ISO 10012 contains quality requirements for a supplier to ensure that measurements are made with the intended accuracy. It also contains guidance on the implementation of the requirements and specifies the main feature of the confirmation system to be used for a supplier's equipment.[7] The section is applicable to measuring equipment used in the demonstration of compliance with a specification but does not apply to other items of measuring equipment. This part of ISO 10012 does not deal exclusively with other elements that might affect measurement results, such as methods of measurement, competence of personnel, and so on. These are dealt with more specifically in other international standards.[8]

5. ISO/FDIS 13485-2003, *Quality Management Systems—Medical Devices—System Requirements for Regulatory Purposes.* This international standard specifies requirements for a quality management system for those organizations that need to demonstrate their ability to provide medical devices that consistently meet customer requirements and regulatory requirements applicable to medical devices and related services.[9] It is important to note that it is not the intent of this standard to stereotype calibration system requirements among individual suppliers. This standard's primary purpose is to present basic concepts that, when properly implemented, will allow a supplier to develop, implement, and maintain a calibration system that is tailored to meet specific needs and expectations relating to a purchase agreement between first and second parties associated with products or services solicited or offered.

Producers of medical devices and others responsible for the administrative application of contract quality requirements must use instruments of known accuracy. There are 10 important issues that must be considered when producing a calibration system for medical devices in accordance with ISO 13485:2003, clause 7.6. Readers will find guidance within this book to address calibration issues referenced in ISO 13485:2003:

Issue	Section (page)
1. Monitoring and measurement to be undertaken and the monitoring and measuring devices needed to provide evidence of conformity to product to determine requirements	"Product Observation Records for M&TE" in chapter 5 (p. 84–90); "The Importance of Establishing a Consistent Calibration System—6. Product or Service Verification Stations" in chapter 1 (p. 10)

Continued

Continued

Issue	Section (page)
2. Documentation of procedures	"Calibration Procedures" in chapter 2 (p. 26–29); "Calibration Procedures for M&TE" in chapter 5 (p. 84–89)
3. Calibration or verification of measuring instruments at specified intervals or prior to use	"Intervals of Calibration" in chapter 2 (p. 23–24); "Intervals of Confirmation" in chapter 6 (p. 117–18)
4. Adjustment of calibration intervals	"Intervals of Confirmation" in chapter 6 (p. 117–18)
5. Identification of calibration status	"Calibration Status" in chapter 2 (p. 46)
6. Safeguarding calibration results from adjustments	"Sealing for Integrity" in chapter 6 (p. 117)
7. Protection of instruments during handling	"Storage and Handling" in chapter 2 (p. 47) and chapter 6 (p. 119)
8. Assessment and documentation of the validity of previous results when equipment is found not to conform to requirements	"Out-of-Tolerance Conditions" in chapter 2 (p. 37–38, 42); "Metrology Deficiency Report," "Nonconforming Product Report," and Figure 5.11 in chapter 5 (p. 91)
9. Appropriate action to be undertaken on the equipment and any product affected by nonconformity	"The Importance of Establishing a Consistent Calibration System—9. Corrective Action" in chapter 1 (p. 11); "Nonconforming Measuring Equipment" in chapter 6 (p. 114); and "Ten-Element Checklist—5. Nonconforming Products and Services" (p. 91, 93, 95)
10. Documentation of the results of calibration and verification	"Application of Records" in chapter 2 (p. 46); "Records" in chapter 6 (p. 109); Figure 2.16 in chapter 2 (p. 38)

The establishment of calibration intervals can also be supported with the application of repeatability and reproducibility (R&R) techniques. This topic is covered exceptionally well in Bill Wortman's *CQE Primer: The Quality Engineer Primer.*[10]

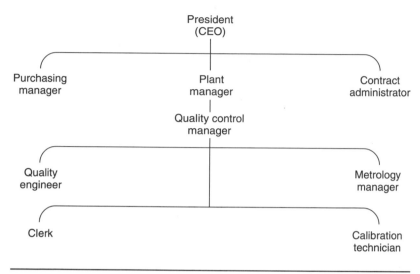

Figure 2.1   A typical organizational structure.

ELEMENTS OF A CALIBRATION SYSTEM

Organizational Structure

Like many other production issues that influence quality, the analysis of a calibration system begins with an understanding of the organization. Clear lines of communication, responsibility, and reporting enhance the capabilities of the contractor to effectively establish, and more important, carry out calibration responsibilities. The organizational structure is beneficial when it is depicted, at a minimum, with hierarchical relationships apparent (see Figure 2.1).

Responsibilities

The responsibilities of the metrology department include the following:

- Preparation of the calibration system description
- Preparation or acquisition of calibration procedures
- Control of the system
- Calibration of measuring equipment

- Identification and correction of out-of-tolerance conditions

- Control of customer-furnished measuring equipment

- Performance of calibration audits

- Support of the purchasing manager

- Control and maintenance of company-designed measuring equipment

- Maintenance of calibration records

- Compliance with established calibration frequencies

- Proper storage and handling of the M&TE

Responsibilities for managing the metrology system are normally divided among QA personnel as follows:

Function	Responsible Individual(s)
Management of policy procedures (system description)	QC manager and/or a designated representative
Management of calibration procedures	QC manager and/or a designated representative
Control of the system	QC manager
Management of calibration of equipment	Metrology department and/or an independent calibration laboratory
Correction of out-of- tolerance conditions	QC manager and/or a designated representative
Control of customer-furnished equipment	Calibration technician as required by contract requirements
Calibration audits	QC manager or a designated representative
Support to the purchasing manager	QC manager
Control of company-designed measuring equipment	QC manager with support from quality engineering
Maintenance of calibration records	Calibration technician
Compliance with established calibration frequencies	Calibration technician
Management of storage and handling	Calibration technician and the user of the instruments

Planning

The planning process begins with a prompt review of the proposed contract (solicitation), the contract award, and the technical data package. If there is ambiguity or if differences of opinion exist between the customer and the supplier concerning contract quality requirements and if clarification cannot be accomplished via telephone or correspondence, then a post-award conference between the supplier and customer's QA representatives might be required. A post-award orientation aids both customer and supplier to achieve a clear and mutual understanding of all contract requirements and identify and resolve potential problems.[11]

When contract quality requirements are established and made known to the QC manager by the contract administrator, inspection and calibration planning can begin. One recommended method for communicating contract quality requirements is to establish a master requirements list. The list is prepared for each product or assembly and requires modification only when there are significant changes to the product design or other contract quality requirements (see Figures 2.2 and 2.3).

1. Date _____				
2. Part name _____		3. Part number _____		
4. Characteristic code number	5. Characteristic identification	6. Measuring device (MD)	7. MD identification number	8. MD code number
_____	_____	_____	_____	_____
_____	_____	_____	_____	_____
_____	_____	_____	_____	_____
_____	_____	_____	_____	_____
_____	_____	_____	_____	_____
_____	_____	_____	_____	_____
_____	_____	_____	_____	_____
9. Prepared by		10. Title		11. Date
_____		_____		_____

Figure 2.2 Master requirements list.

Block number	Action
1. Date	Enter as appropriate.
2. Part name	Enter the name of the product that is to be inspected.
3. Part number	Enter the product part number.
4. Characteristic code number	a. Enter drawing dimension code number.
	b. When a specification applies, enter the applicable specification paragraph number or its code number.
	c. When special contract quality requirements apply, enter the applicable contract section paragraph or its code number.
5. Characteristic identification	Enter all of the product parameters.
	a. For drawings, enter actual dimensions.
	b. For specifications, enter specification number, applicable section, and paragraph number.
	c. For special contract quality requirements, enter contract section and paragraph number.
6. Measuring device (MD)	Enter the instrument that will be used to check the respective characteristic.
7. MD identification number	Enter the identification number assigned to the measuring instrument.
8. MD code number	Enter the code number (assigned by the quality control manager or a designated representative) that identifies the measuring instrument.
	This number traces nonconforming products and/or measuring equipment when married with the respective product inspection report.
9. Prepared by	Enter the name of the quality control manager or a designated representative.
10. Title	Enter as appropriate.
11. Date	Enter as appropriate.

Figure 2.3 Instructions for preparing the master requirements list.

Environmental Controls

There are three factors to consider when determining the required extent of environmental controls:

1. The accuracy of measurement standards

2. The accuracy of measuring and test equipment

3. The product tolerances

When there is a clear understanding of instrument accuracy as well as product tolerance requirements, a determination can be made regarding the extent of environmental controls. Establishing environmental controls eliminates potential detrimental conditions that might affect the accuracy and stability of the M&TE and MS. The environmental elements that affect instrument accuracy include:

- Temperature

- Relative humidity

- Dust (particle count)

- Electrical and radio-frequency noise

- Lighting

Intervals of Calibration

Measuring equipment should be calibrated as often as necessary to maintain prescribed accuracies. Calibrations can be accomplished on an established frequency or prior to use. Where there is sporadic production, the "prior-to-use" method is recommended. When production is continuous, the establishment of calibration frequencies (intervals) is recommended. Calibration frequencies are usually delegated to one of the following:

- *A supplier's calibration laboratory.* Calibration intervals are normally established within a company's own calibration laboratory by a metrology manager or the manager's designated calibration technician(s). However, in deference to costs, particularly when expertise is questionable, there are situations in which this function is shared with an independent calibration laboratory.

- *An independent calibration laboratory.* Intervals of calibration should be delegated to an independent laboratory when a history of objective calibration data is readily available.

• *The instrument manufacturer.* An instrument manufacturer can provide instructions regarding the establishment of intervals of calibration. End users of the instrument are cautioned to establish calibration intervals that are based on the degree of usage.

Calibration records play an important role in the establishment of calibration intervals and interval adjustments. The justification of interval adjustments is predicated on data generated during previous calibrations. (See chapter 7 for additional discussion of the effect of intervals of calibration.) When inspection records indicate that the inspection equipment requires frequent adjustments, the interval should be shortened and the pertinent data should be evaluated to determine the impact on out-of-tolerance conditions. Intervals can be lengthened if the results of previous calibrations provide positive indications that the accuracy of the equipment will not be adversely affected.

When no calibration history has been generated for a particular measuring device or when contractual requirements are silent regarding the application of a specific calibration interval for a given instrument, a track record must be established before deciding on a particular frequency of calibration. Under these conditions the following steps should be taken:

1. Calibrate the instrument prior to use for one week. If the history of calibration shows that no adjustments were required, proceed to next step.

2. Calibrate the instrument weekly for four weeks. If a favorable history prevails, proceed to next step.

3. Calibrate the instrument once a month for six months. If after this period, the records indicate no out-of-tolerance conditions, proceed to next step.

4. Calibrate the instrument every six months for one year. If the calibration record shows that no out-of-tolerance conditions are in evidence, calibrate the instrument once a year.

5. When a significant out-of-tolerance condition (one that adversely affects an established calibration interval) becomes evident, return to step 2, 3, or 4.

A recall system must be in place to ensure that calibrations are performed within specified intervals. The establishment and maintenance of a recall/location record is one method of ensuring that calibration schedules are met (see Figures 2.4 and 2.5).

1. Nomenclature _____

2. Identification number _____   3. Instruction number _____

4. Calibration frequency _____

5. Item location _____

_____

6. Date recalled	7. Calibration date	8. Assigned to	9. Date in service	10. Assigned by	11. Remarks
___	___	___	___	___	___
___	___	___	___	___	___
___	___	___	___	___	___
___	___	___	___	___	___
___	___	___	___	___	___
___	___	___	___	___	___
___	___	___	___	___	___
___	___	___	___	___	___

Figure 2.4   Measuring equipment recall/location record form.

A temporary extension of calibration due dates may be authorized only when a favorable in-tolerance history is in evidence. Unless otherwise authorized by the customer, no shipments should be made to the customer until the pertinent measuring equipment has been found to be in tolerance and calibration results are documented on the respective form furnished for this purpose.

Calibration Procedures

Written methods or procedures for calibrating M&TE and MS must be provided by the contractor to eliminate possible measurement inaccuracies due

Block number	Action
1. Nomenclature	Enter the name of the instrument that is used within the calibration system.
2. Identification number	Enter the number that identifies the instrument.
3. Instruction number	Enter the instruction number shown in respective calibration procedure.
4. Calibration frequency	Enter the established calibration frequency.
5. Item location	Enter the calibration laboratory or inspection station where the measuring equipment is located as well as those locations at an independent laboratory or at the subcontractor's facility, when applicable.
6. Date recalled	Enter as appropriate.
7. Calibration date	Enter the date calibrated.
8. Assigned to	Enter the person and/or department that the equipment is assigned to.
9. Date in service	Enter as appropriate.
10. Assigned by	Enter the calibration technician's signature or initials.
11. Remarks	Enter as appropriate.

Figure 2.5 Instructions for preparing the measuring equipment recall/location record form.

to differences in techniques, environmental conditions, or choice of higher-level standards. The preparation of a calibration procedure is based on functional and physical characteristics of the product design. A detailed review and analysis of drawings, specifications, and special contract quality requirements and related product characteristics and their special tolerances will lead to the identification of the M&TE that will be required to check the product. Figure 2.6 reflects the steps that lead to the application of required calibration procedures.

There are three main sources of calibration procedures:

1. Procedures compiled by the product manufacturer

2. Published standards

3. Instrument manufacturers' recommended calibration procedures

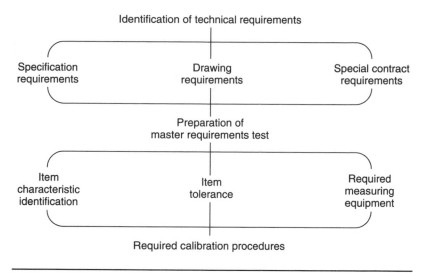

Identification of technical requirements

| Specification requirements | Drawing requirements | Special contract requirements |

Preparation of
master requirements test

| Item characteristic identification | Item tolerance | Required measuring equipment |

Required calibration procedures

Figure 2.6   Steps that lead to the application of required calibration procedures.

When published standards or the instrument manufacturer's recommended procedures are not available to the product manufacturer, the manufacturer must prepare its own calibration procedures.

Product Manufacturer's Calibration Procedures

The product manufacturer's calibration procedures should address the factors shown in Figures 2.7 and 2.8. These procedures must be upgraded when conditions warrant.

Published Standards

Published standards are available from participating members of the Government and Industry Data Exchange Program (GIDEP). You can write to: Operations Center, Naval Weapons Station, Seal Beach, Corona, CA 91720.

GIDEP was established to conserve time, personnel, and money by eliminating redundant technical effort among government and industry design, research, development, engineering, and procurement programs. Participation in GIDEP may be a contractual requirement. Organizations not having contracts that specify mandatory participation in GIDEP can participate voluntarily by exchanging data applicable to the metrology data

1. Original/date _____   2. Revision/date _____

3. Instrument
   nomenclature _____   4. Calibration
                                        procedure number _____

5. Instrument   6. Instrument   7. Instrument
   accuracy   range   discrimination

   _____   _____   _____

   _____   _____   _____

8. Measurement standards (MS)

   _____

   _____

9. Procedure

   _____

   _____

10. Name (preparer)/title/date _____

Figure 2.7 Calibration procedure form.

Block number	Action
1. Original/date	If the procedure was prepared first hand, enter a check mark in the "original" block and the date that the procedure was prepared.
2. Revision/date	When a change is made to the calibration procedure, enter a check mark in the "revision" block and the date that the change was made.
3. Instrument nomenclature	Enter as appropriate.
4. Calibration procedure number	Enter a number that identifies the procedure.
5. Instrument accuracy	Enter the accuracy (discrimination) of the instrument that is to be calibrated.

Continued

Figure 2.8 Instructions for preparing calibration procedures.

Continued

Block number	Action
6. Instrument range	Enter the range of the instrument that is to be calibrated. Example: If a zero to one inch micrometer is to be calibrated over its entire range, then enter "0–1."
	If the instrument is to be calibrated from zero to one-half inch, then enter "0–.500."
7. Instrument discrimination	Enter the smallest scale division of the instrument that is to be calibrated.
8. Measurement standards (MS)	a. Enter the name(s) of the MS that will be used to calibrate the instrument.
	b. Enter the accuracy of measurement standards.
	c. Remember to select only MSs with a higher level of accuracy.
9. Procedure	Enter a step-by-step procedure that will satisfy calibration requirements for the instrument that is under calibration.
10. Name (preparer)/title/date	Enter as appropriate.

Figure 2.8 Instructions for preparing calibration procedures.

bank and by providing annual reports of program benefits. Reports must be submitted at least once a year to continue participation in the program.

Instrument Manufacturer's Calibration Procedures

The instrument manufacturer's recommended calibration procedures are normally furnished with the purchased instrument. Occasionally, these procedures might have to be ordered under separate cover. See Figure 2.9 for an example of an instrument manufacturer's calibration procedure.

ACCURACY OF THE MS AND M&TE

The selection of the M&TE begins with knowing the product tolerances of items produced and the accuracy requirements of related M&TE. The decision to calibrate the selected M&TE or MS in-house or use an outside source

BTG-1 Digital Gage Amplifier

1. 0–9, CLR,-	Used input information.
2. MODE	Select probe A only, probe B only, or probe A and probe B together. The mode light will indicate which probes are selected.
3. +/–	Changes the sign of the selected probe. Not valid when both probes are selected. When inputting information as in *mean, gain, offset,* or *message,* it allows entering a negative sign or dash.
4. E/M	Select readings in inches or millimeters (English/metric).
5. XMIT	Transmits information in display over RS-232 interface.
6. HOLD	Freezes the current reading. To read new sizes, press the *hold* button again.
7. PRINT	Prints the information in the display. Sizes are right-justified and messages are left-justified.
8. ADV	Advances the printer.
9. ENTER	Enters new information into the selected register.
10. RANGE	Selects the range of the amplifier. The range lights will indicate which range is selected.
11. ZERO	Allows zeroing readings to a zero master.
	a. Set up zero master.
	b. Press *zero.*
12. MEAN	Allows setting a mean size.
	a. Set up zero master.
	b. Press *zero.*
	c. Press *mean.*
	d. Input Mean size using CLR, +/–, ., and 0–9.
	e. Press *enter* to store mean size.
	f. To clear a mean size, use the sequence *mean,* CLR, and *enter.*

Figure 2.9   A sample calibration procedure—keyboard functions.

such as an independent calibration laboratory is predicated on the volume of work, costs, technical capabilities, and the availability of facilities and equipment. For example, if the calibrations are infrequent, then a study should be made to assess the cost of performing these calibrations in-house as compared to using the services of an independent calibration laboratory.

When there is a large volume of work that requires continuous repair and calibration of inspection equipment and M&TE, most companies use their own metrology specialists and their own calibration laboratory. However, in the case of both infrequent and continuous calibrations, many producers of products and services rely on both internal and external sources to calibrate and maintain the accuracy of their M&TE.

No two parts can be made exactly alike. This conclusion is shared by the design engineer, product manufacturer, and metrology manager in deference to interchangeability. To ensure interchangeability of mating parts, the design engineer assigns a tolerance to product parameters. This tolerance allows for the variations inherent in the manufactured product which are attributed to machine capabilities, people capabilities, and associated processes.

The calibration technician considers the product tolerance when selecting the best measuring equipment to verify product quality. Product tolerances can be referenced in a unilateral or bilateral direction:

- Unilateral: A variation that is permitted in one direction from a specified dimension (see Figure 2.10)

- Bilateral: A variation that is permitted in two directions from a specified dimension (see Figure 2.11)

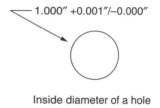

Inside diameter of a hole

Figure 2.10   Product tolerance in a unilateral direction.

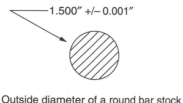

Outside diameter of a round bar stock

Figure 2.11   Product tolerance in a bilateral direction.

When instrument calibration is accomplished, the technician focuses on the discrimination of the MS and related M&TE, as well as the accuracy ratio between the two. When determining the adequacy of the MS and M&TE, the technician monitors the potential measurement error and the area of uncertainty that exists on either side of every reading. The technician then reduces the acceptable range of an acceptable reading by the prescribed tolerance of the measuring device (comparator). The technician allows for:

- The limitations inherent in the construction of M&TE

- The environmental conditions under which measurements are made

- The different ways the technician uses and reads measuring equipment

A high accuracy ratio between the comparator (MS or M&TE) and the item checked (M&TE or product) will provide a high degree of measurement confidence. Conversely, a low accuracy ratio will reflect a low degree of measurement confidence. Potential measurement error can be minimized with the proper selection of higher-level accuracy ratios between the MS and M&TE (see Table 2.1).

With the exception of those conditions in which state-of-the-art limitations preclude the use of accuracy ratios greater than 1:1, the selection of accuracy ratios between the comparator and the item that is being calibrated or inspected should be greater than 2:1 and preferably greater than 4:1. The examples shown in Figures 2.12, 2.13, 2.14, and 2.15 as well as Table 2.2 pertain to measurements that fall within an item's (instrument or product) tolerance range and are intended to show the impact that areas of uncertainty (or areas of acceptance) have on instrument adequacy.

A 1:1 accuracy ratio will reflect a 100 percent area of uncertainty; therefore *all* measurements that fall within an item's tolerance range will land in an area of uncertainty. Rejecting is normal when a measured value for those items falls outside of allowable tolerances. It is important to note that a 1:1 accuracy ratio might or might not indicate that items calibrated under these conditions are in conformance with prescribed tolerances. A 1:1 accuracy ratio might not provide the required measurement confidence. In addition, it might lead to material review board (MRB) actions and unanticipated quality costs. An MRB consists of technical representatives employed by a product manufacturer whose primary responsibility is to determine or recommend the proper disposition of material referred to them.

Table 2.1 Impact of accuracy ratios.

Ratio	Area of Acceptance	Area of Uncertainty
1:1	0%	100%
2:1	50%	50%
4:1	75%	25%
10:1	90%	10%

Factors for determining accuracy ratios are:

R = Ratio

PT = Product tolerance

M&TAT = Measuring and test equipment accuracy tolerance

SAT = Secondary standard accuracy tolerance

PAT = Primary standard accuracy tolerance

Ratio selection:

a. Product manufacturer's prevailing (tightest) product tolerance = 0.005"

b. M&TAT = 0.001"

c. SAT = 0.0001"

d. PAT = 0.000004"

Ratio between M&TE tolerance and product tolerance:

$$R = \frac{PT}{M\&TAT} = \frac{0.005"}{0.001"}$$
$$= 5:1 (nominal) = ratio$$

Ratio between secondary measurement standard and measuring and test equipment:

$$R = \frac{M\&TAT}{SAT} = \frac{0.001"}{0.0001"}$$
$$= 10:1 \ (nominal) = ratio$$

Ratio between primary standard and secondary standard:

$$R = \frac{SAT}{PAT} = \frac{0.001"}{0.000004"}$$
$$= 25:1 = ratio$$

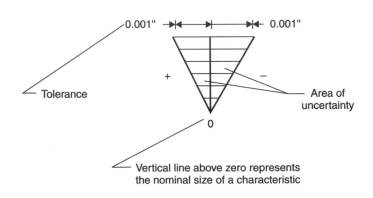

Item (instrument or product) tolerance = +/– 0.001"

$$\frac{\text{Tolerance (+/–)}}{\text{ratio}} = \frac{T}{R} = \frac{0.001"}{1} = 0.001 \quad \begin{array}{l}\text{(Discrimination}\\\text{of comparator)}\end{array}$$

Comparator

0.001"   0.001"

\+   –

Tolerance   Area of
                                   uncertainty

0

Vertical line above zero represents
the nominal size of a characteristic

Figure 2.12   Example of a 1:1 accuracy ratio.

A 4:1 accuracy ratio will reflect a 75 percent area of acceptance and a 25 percent area of uncertainty. A 10:1 accuracy ratio will reflect a 90 percent area of acceptance and a 10 percent area of uncertainty. The use of a ratio of 10:1 or greater will provide greater measurement confidence and will reduce potential measurement errors.

When measurements fall within the area of acceptance, measurement confidence can be achieved. However, when measurements fall within an area of uncertainty, a decision to accept or reject a measurement might be questionable. Measuring equipment with a high level of accuracy will greatly assist the technician in making the right decision to accept or reject measured readings.

The technician must make sure that accuracy ratios between the M&TE and the product tolerance and between the MS and M&TE are adequate for the purpose intended. A ratio greater than 4:1 is acceptable. However, a ratio of 10:1 or greater is recommended whenever possible. When measurements fall within an area of uncertainty, a decision must be made as to its impact on out-of-tolerance conditions.

$$\text{Tolerance} = \frac{T}{R} = \frac{0.001"}{4} = 0.00025" \begin{matrix} \text{(Discrimination} \\ \text{of comparator)} \end{matrix}$$

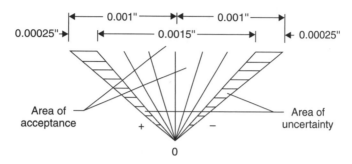

Comparator

Comments:

a. The area of uncertainty is equal to the accuracy of the comparator.

b. When measurements fall in the area of uncertainty, a determination must be made as to its impact in allowable tolerances.

   For example: An allowable product tolerance for a one-inch diameter bar stock is +/– 0.001":

Actual measurement	= 1.001"
Area of uncertainty	= 0.00025"
Discrimination allowance	= ± 0.00025"

   Therefore . . .
   The acceptable reading is considered
   to be between 1.00075" and 1.00125"

Conclusion is that the measurement can either be accepted at 1.00075" or rejected at 1.00125".

Figure 2.13   Example of a 4:1 accuracy ratio.

Item (instrument or product) tolerance = 0.001"

$$\frac{\text{Tolerance (+/−)}}{\text{ratio}} = \frac{T}{R} = \frac{0.001"}{10} = 0.0001 \begin{array}{l}\text{(Discrimination}\\\text{of comparator)}\end{array}$$

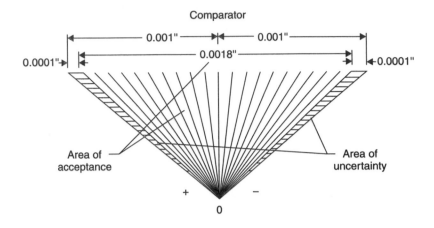

Comments:

a. The area of uncertainty is equal to the accuracy of the comparator.

b. When measurements fall in the area of uncertainty, a determination must be made as to its impact on allowable tolerances.

> For example: An allowable product tolerance for a one-inch diameter bar stock is +/− 0.001":

Actual measurement	= 1.001"
Area of uncertainty	= 0.0001"
Discrimination allowance	= ± 0.0001"

> Therefore . . .
> The acceptable reading is considered
> to be between 1.0009" and 1.0011"

Conclusion is that the measurement can either be accepted at 1.0009" or rejected at 1.0011".

Figure 2.14 Example of a 10:1 accuracy ratio.

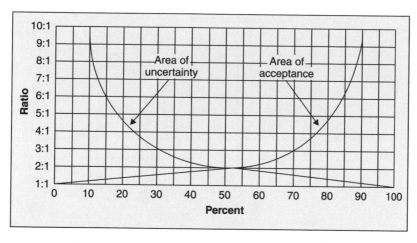

Figure 2.15   Representative curve for a product tolerance of 0.001".

Table 2.2   Accuracy ratios between product tolerance and M&TE.

Ratio	Comparator Discrimination	Area of Uncertainty	Area of Acceptance
1:1	0.001000"	100%	0%
2:1	0.000500"	50%	50%
3:1	0.000333"	33%	67%
4:1	0.000250"	25%	75%
5:1	0.000200"	20%	80%
6:1	0.000167"	16%	84%
7:1	0.000143"	14%	86%
8:1	0.000125"	13%	87%
9:1	0.000110"	11%	89%
10:1	0.000100"	10%	90%

OUT-OF-TOLERANCE CONDITIONS

In-tolerance and out-of-tolerance conditions are determined by the review of feedback data furnished by the calibration agency. Examples of forms that are used by the calibrating agency to record calibration data are found in Figure 2.16, Figure 2.17, and Figure 2.18. The calibration agency can be

Calibration Record

Instrument _____

Model _____   Location _____

I.D. no. _____   Accuracy _____

Procedure no. _____   Discrimination _____

Calibration freq. _____   Tamper-proof   ☐ Yes   ☐ No

Other _____

Date calibrated	Due date	Calibration technician	Work performance								
			Characteristic identification								
			Measured value								

Figure 2.16   An example of a manufacturer's calibration record.

the product manufacturer's calibration laboratory, an independent calibration laboratory, the National Institute of Standards and Technology (NIST), or a combination thereof. Calibration data that is used to assess in-tolerance and out-of-tolerance conditions is provided by all of these organizations. Generally speaking, product manufacturers generate calibration data associated with

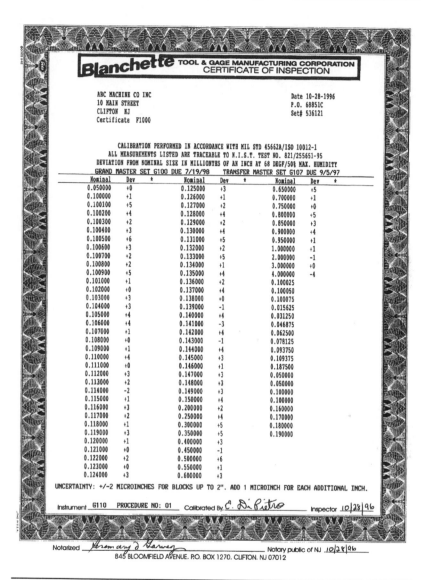

Blanchette TOOL & GAGE MANUFACTURING CORPORATION
CERTIFICATE OF INSPECTION

ABC MACHINE CO INC
10 MAIN STREET
CLIFTON NJ
Certificate F1000

Date 10-28-1996
P.O. 68851C
Set# 536121

CALIBRATION PERFORMED IN ACCORDANCE WITH MIL STD 45662A/ISO 10012-1
ALL MEASUREMENTS LISTED ARE TRACEABLE TO N.I.S.T. TEST NO. 821/255651-95
DEVIATION FROM NOMINAL SIZE IN MILLIONTHS OF AN INCH AT 68 DEGF/50% MAX. HUMIDITY
GRAND MASTER SET G100 DUE 7/19/98   TRANSFER MASTER SET G107 DUE 9/5/97

Nominal	Dev	*	Nominal	Dev	*	Nominal	Dev	*
0.050000	+0		0.125000	+3		0.650000	+5	
0.100000	+1		0.126000	+1		0.700000	+1	
0.100100	+5		0.127000	+2		0.750000	+0	
0.100200	+4		0.128000	+4		0.800000	+5	
0.100300	+2		0.129000	+2		0.850000	+3	
0.100400	+3		0.130000	+4		0.900000	+4	
0.100500	+6		0.131000	+5		0.950000	+1	
0.100600	+3		0.132000	+2		1.000000	+1	
0.100700	+2		0.133000	+5		2.000000	-1	
0.100800	+2		0.134000	+1		3.000000	+0	
0.100900	+5		0.135000	+4		4.000000	-4	
0.101000	+1		0.136000	+2		0.100025		
0.102000	+0		0.137000	+4		0.100050		
0.103000	+3		0.138000	+0		0.100075		
0.104000	+3		0.139000	-1		0.015625		
0.105000	+4		0.140000	+4		0.031250		
0.106000	+4		0.141000	-3		0.046875		
0.107000	+1		0.142000	+4		0.062500		
0.108000	+0		0.143000	-1		0.078125		
0.109000	+1		0.144000	+4		0.093750		
0.110000	+4		0.145000	+3		0.109375		
0.111000	+0		0.146000	+1		0.187500		
0.112000	+3		0.147000	+3		0.050000		
0.113000	+2		0.148000	+3		0.050000		
0.114000	-2		0.149000	+3		0.100000		
0.115000	+1		0.150000	+3		0.100000		
0.116000	+3		0.200000	+2		0.160000		
0.117000	+2		0.250000	+4		0.170000		
0.118000	+1		0.300000	+5		0.180000		
0.119000	+3		0.350000	+5		0.190000		
0.120000	+1		0.400000	+3				
0.121000	+0		0.450000	-1				
0.122000	+2		0.500000	+6				
0.123000	+0		0.550000	+1				
0.124000	+3		0.600000	+3				

UNCERTAINTY: +/-2 MICROINCHES FOR BLOCKS UP TO 2". ADD 1 MICROINCH FOR EACH ADDITIONAL INCH.

Instrument G110   PROCEDURE NO: 01   Calibrated By C. Di Pietro   Inspector 10/28/96

Notarized _Rosemary J Garvey_   Notary public of NJ 10/28/96
845 BLOOMFIELD AVENUE. P.O. BOX 1270. CLIFTON. NJ 07012

Figure 2.17 A sample certificate of inspection.   *Continued*

Continued

```
PROCEDURE NO. 01:  GAGE BLOCK INSPECTION  ALL GAGE BLOCKS ARE
CLEANED, DEBURRED AND CHECKED ON DUAL-JET GAGE BLOCK COMPARATORS
G109 OR G110.  AS PER DOCUMENT GGG-G-15C, MEASUREMENT IS TAKEN
AT SPECIFIED REFERENCE POINT, WITH DEVIATION FROM NOMINAL SIZE
SIZE GIVEN IN MILLIONTHS OF AN INCH

THE UNCERTAINTY OF MEASUREMENT FACTOR:  THE UNCERTAINTY OF
MEASUREMENT IS +/-2 MICROINCHES FOR BLOCKS UP TO AND INCLUDING
2 INCHES.  FOR BLOCKS EXCEEDING 2 INCHES, ADD 1 MICROINCH FOR
EACH ADDITIONAL INCH

N.I.S.T. TRACEABILITY NUMBERS:

_____    TEST NO. 821/255651-95.  GRAND MASTER SET G100
         SN 9.2572A+6.  CAL: 7-19-95  DUE: 7-19-98
_____    TRANSFER MASTER SET G107 CAL: 9-5-96  DUE: 9-5-97

_____    TEST NO. 821/253616-94.  WAFER MASTER SET G103/G104/G105
         SN EIG1686/ML05/JIK1687.  CAL: 8-29-94  DUE: 8-29-97

_____    TEST NO. 821/252163-93.  LONG RANGE MASTER SET G106
         SN 51280.16.  CAL: 1-20-94  DUE: 1-20-97

_____    TEST NO. 821/254855-95.  METRIC MASTER SET G101/G102
         SN 3876.1.  CAL: 11-28-95  DUE: 11-28-98
```

Figure 2.17   A sample certificate of inspection.

inspection equipment, M&TE, and some instruments that they classify as their measurement standards. An independent calibration will calibrate all other measurement standards and working instruments that a product manufacturer has elected to be calibrated by an outside calibration source.

Feedback data are reviewed and analyzed by the metrology manager or a designated representative at the time of calibration or shortly thereafter to determine:

- The adequacy of established calibration intervals

- Whether there is a need to adjust calibration intervals

- Whether there is a need to modify established calibration procedures

- The adequacy of the calibration system and equipment reliability

- The identification of out-of-tolerance equipment and the prevention of the use of that equipment until the reported deficiency has been corrected

Report of Calibration

For: *# of blocks*

Serial no. _____

Submitted by: *Company name*
              Address

These gage blocks were compared with the standards of the United States. The comparison process employs electromechanical comparators and four gage blocks (two standards and two test blocks) in a least squares intercomparison schedule designed to eliminate the effects of thermal drift.

This process together with its statistical analysis constitutes a continuous measurement assurance program maintained at NIST to ensure that realistic uncertainty values are assigned to the length determinations. Details of the process are covered in NBSIR 80-2078, "The NBS Gage Block Calibration Process Using a Measurement Assurance Program," which is considered to be a part of this report.

The deviation in length from the nominal size at 20 degrees Celsius (68 degrees F) is given on the following pages along with total uncertainty for each gage block.

These blocks were compared with similar blocks from NIST Test No. _____ .

Measurements were made by _____ .

For the director,
National Institute of Standards and Technology

Ralph C. Veale, Group Leader
Dimensional Metrology
Precision Engineering Division
Center for Manufacturing Engineering

Purchase Order No. _____

NIST Test No. _____

Date: _____

Figure 2.18   NIST report of calibration.

Reprinted with permission from NIST, United States Department of Commerce, National Institute of Standards and Technology, Gaithersburg, Maryland 20899.

Out-of-tolerance conditions of MSs and M&TE are placed into three general categories: conditions A, B, and C. The following describes these conditions and their impact on accuracy requirements.

Condition (Ratio between MS and M&TE)	Impact on Accuracy Requirements
A (4:1 to 10:1 or higher)	The adequacy of the MS and M&TE will be satisfactorily maintained. No action is required.
B (2:1 to less than 4:1)	When instrument accuracy deteriorates from Condition A to Condition B, investigate the applicable factors that contribute to this trend toward an out-of-tolerance condition.
C (less than 2:1)	When instrument accuracy deteriorates to Condition C, it will have a major impact on the accuracy requirements of the MS and M&TE. It is a significant condition that will require immediate corrective action. Investigate all of the factors that impact out-of-tolerance conditions. (These factors are referenced later in this chapter.)

When an out-of-tolerance condition prevails, an investigation is required to determine:

- The accuracy of the MS used to calibrate the M&TE

- The adequacy of the M&TE used to check the product

- The adequacy of calibration intervals

- The quality of products accepted in-house as well as the quality of the products shipped to the customers

- The adequacy of the established calibration procedures

Attribute-type instruments such as go/no go gages are considered significantly out-of-tolerance when their dimension sizes exceed the maximum and minimum material limits of a product's feature size. Significant out-of-tolerance conditions must be documented and brought to the attention of the responsible department supervisor for appropriate action. Figure 2.19 provides a sample metrology deficiency report. Figure 2.20 gives instructions on how to prepare that report.

1. To _____

2. From _____

3. Report number _____ 4. Date _____

5. Measuring device _____

6. Identification number _____ 7. Calibration procedure number _____

8. Reply due date _____

9. Signature of requestor _____

10. Out-of-tolerance condition

11. Corrective action as to cause

12. Conclusion: Complaint is justified _____ not justified _____

13. Recommended corrective action

14. Investigator's signature _____

15. Title _____ 16. Date _____

Figure 2.19   Metrology deficiency report.

Block number	Action
1. To	Enter quality control manager, metrology manager, or other (as applicable).
2. From	Enter name of the agency that performed the calibration.
3. Report number	Begin with number one for the first report, two for the second report, etc.
4. Date	Enter as appropriate.
5. Measuring device	Enter the instrument nomenclature.
6. Identification number	Enter as appropriate.
7. Calibration procedure number	Enter number shown in the respective calibration procedure.
8. Reply due date	Enter date established by the requestor.
9. Signature of requestor	Enter as appropriate.
10. Out-of-tolerance condition	Describe observed deficiency in detail. Attach supporting data when necessary.
11. Corrective action as to cause	Identify the cause of the deficiency that created the out-of-tolerance condition.
12. Conclusion	Determine if complaint is justified. Enter appropriate block.
13. Recommended corrective action	a. Recalibrate measuring device using high–action level accuracy standards. b. Upgrade calibration procedures. c. Reinspect the product with measuring equipment of known accuracy. d. Shorten calibration interval. e. Other as appropriate.
14., 15., and 16.	Enter as appropriate.

Figure 2.20   Instructions for preparing the metrology deficiency report.

CALIBRATION SOURCES

There are three main calibration sources. They are:

1. A commercial facility, such as an independent calibration laboratory, whose calibration equipment is certified as being traceable to NIST.

2. A contractor whose calibration is traceable directly to NIST or through an unbroken chain of properly conducted calibrations that are traceable to NIST.

3. NIST, formerly known as the National Bureau of Standards (NBS).

The following information is reprinted with permission from NIST:

On August 23, 1988, the President of the United States signed into law the Omnibus Trade and Competitiveness Act of 1988, including the Technology Competitiveness Act. The Act has created the National Institute of Standards and Technology (NIST) from the National Bureau of Standards (NBS).

Our new name reflects the increased responsibility assigned to our agency to support and enhance the technological competitiveness of U.S. industry, as well as our traditional function of providing measurements, calibrations, and quality assurance standards vital to U.S. industry.

The new law has provided a challenge as well as innovative mechanisms for NIST to aid industry. The institute is instructed to create a series of "Regional Centers for the Transfer of Manufacturing Technology" that will be affiliated with nonprofit institutions or organizations. NIST is also to create a program to provide assistance and make federal technology available to state and local technology programs and technology extension services.

An "Advance Technology Program" will be established to encourage the commercialization of high-technology products. NIST will also support a Department of Commerce Clearinghouse for State and Local Initiatives on Productivity, Technology, and Innovation, providing technical and analytical help to state and local officials making decisions on technology policy. Not all of these functions, however, are currently funded. Those services and research areas for which NBS has been known in the past will continue under NIST. In particular, our Standard Reference Materials, Standard Reference Data Programs, and calibration services will continue to serve the needs of American industry and science.

APPLICATION OF RECORDS

Recording the functions of quality is one of the best methods of providing objective quality evidence. Records are made of work accomplished, compliance with work instructions, and noncompliance with work instructions. Records that control and maintain the calibration system include the following:

Record	Purpose
Item identification	Tag or label instruments
Item history	Standard form (record of calibration)
Out-of-tolerance conditions	Standard form (triggers the need for the adjustment of calibration policies and/or procedures)
Calibration procedures	Step-by-step procedure to eliminate possible measurement inaccuracies

CALIBRATION STATUS

Calibration status is accomplished by the use of tags, labels, or codes. The selected method should, at a minimum, identify the date, month, and year that the instrument was calibrated as well as the calibration due date. Labels should be attached to the instrument. When it is impractical to attach a label to the instrument, it can be attached to the instrument's container.

Limited-use M&TE should be identified as such; information about the range of the instrument's use should be included. Obsolete and out-of-service instruments should be identified as such and stored apart from active equipment. Uncalibrated instruments should not be used.

CONTROL OF SUBCONTRACTOR CALIBRATION

The selection of capable subcontractors is the responsibility of both the purchasing and QC managers. The purchasing manager is responsible for procuring the supplies and services that are required for the support of a manufactured product. The purchasing manager coordinates the proposed subcontractor with the QC manager and alerts suppliers of pertinent calibration system requirements. The QC manager ensures that subcontracted supplies and services conform to purchase order requirements. The QC manager is also responsible for the review of suppliers' quality functions at intervals consistent with complexity and accuracy requirements of products and services offered by the suppliers.

STORAGE AND HANDLING

M&TE should be placed in containers or wrapped in moisture-free barrier material and placed in suitable bins to ensure that the equipment maintains the required level of accuracy. The equipment should also be carefully handled during movement and use.

MAINTENANCE OF POLICIES AND PROCEDURES

QA personnel must have ready access to contract and product design changes. If policies and procedures are to be satisfactorily maintained, QA personnel must know of changes in technical requirements and other contract quality requirements to continually evaluate and determine the impact that those changes have on established policies and procedures. Timely and effective changes to established policies and procedures ensure that maximum effort can be directed to the satisfactory maintenance of an established calibration system description.

Management must reward and recognize employees who successfully apply a calibration system. When policies and procedures are written so that support documentation is in place and where an ongoing system for evaluation of a calibration system is maintained, the results will create:

- A foundation for good quality

- A reinforcement of measurement confidence

- The enhancement of the quality expectations of the customer

Most of all, a well-maintained calibration system will have a positive impact on the quality of products and services offered to the customer.

ENDNOTES

1. ANSI/ASQC M1-1996, *American National Standard for Calibration Systems,* clause 1, 1.
2. ANSI/ISO 17025-1999, *General Requirements for the Competence of Testing and Calibration Laboratories*, clause 1.1
3. Ibid.
4. ANSI/NCSL Z540-1-1994, *Calibration Laboratories and Measuring and Test Equipment—General Requirements,* clause 1.1, 1.
5. Ibid, clause 1.2, 1.
6. Ibid, clause 1.3, 1.
7. ISO 10012-1-1992, *Quality Assurance Requirements for Measuring Equipment—Part 1: Metrological Confirmation System for Measuring Equipment,* clauses 1.1 and 1.2, 1.
8. Ibid, clause 1.3, 1.
9. ISO 13485:2003, *Quality Management Systems—Medical Devices—System Requirements for Regulatory Purposes.*
10. B. Wortman, *CQE Primer: The Quality Engineer Primer,* 6th ed. (West Terre Haute: Quality Council of Indiana, 2000).
11. U.S. Department of Defense, General Services Administration, and National Aeronautics and Space Administration, *Federal Acquisition Regulation,* part 42, clause 42.501 (1995).

3

Metrology Audit

The metrological function shall be defined by the organization. Top management of the organization shall ensure the availability of necessary resources to establish and maintain the metrological function. The metrological function may be a single department or distributed throughout the organization. The management of the metrological function shall establish, document, and maintain the measurement management system and continually improve its effectiveness.[1]

AUDITORS

Metrology audits are predicated on need. An audit can be performed on only one, a few, or all of the applicable elements of an adopted calibration system standard. Internal audits are conducted to verify that documented policy, procedures, and processes are being followed. Internal audits also support top management in its attempt to improve established procedures and processes.

Metrology audits should be performed by certified or experienced QA specialists who do not have specific responsibilities in the area audited. The auditors should be familiar with the appropriate portions of a documented quality plan and associated procedures and processes. Audit responsibilities can be delegated by the QA director to a member of his or her staff or to an independent consultant. However, if the audit is complex in nature, the audit responsibilities can be delegated to a team of specialists, consisting of the QA director, quality engineer, metrology manager, and calibration technician. External metrology audits are conducted in situations in which a prime contractor decides to delegate some or all of the metrology functions to an independent calibration laboratory.

REVIEW OF POLICIES AND PROCEDURES

A calibration system audit begins with the review of established policies and procedures followed by the verification of those policies and procedures at the respective calibration sites and inspection stations. If documented policies and procedures are unavailable at the time of the scheduled audit, or if they are considered inadequate, a report of these findings should be brought to the attention of the responsible department supervisor. The audit team must then terminate the calibration audit but continue to perform an audit of operations (when this action is determined by the team leader to be in the best interest of the QA process). The calibration audit must be rescheduled after the required documentation is in place and put into operation. The timely review of documented policies and procedures is a "table setting" operation to ensure that all requirements of a calibration system have been addressed by the supplier and that they are included in a master quality plan.

DEGREE OF APPLICATION

After the system description is found to be acceptable and in place, a determination will be made as to the degree of audit application. Sixteen elements form the basis for preparing audit checklists. These 16 elements are provided for information purposes only. They are generic in nature and should be used in an audit checklist only if they apply to a specific contract quality requirement, a quality plan, or an associated policy, procedure, or process. The elements are:

1. Intervals of calibration
2. Out-of-tolerance conditions
3. Calibration system requirements
4. Adequacy of MSs

5. Environmental controls

6. Calibration procedures

7. Calibration sources

8. Application of records

9. Calibration status

10. Control of subcontractor calibration

11. Purchaser-supplied M&TE

12. Storage and handling

13. Inventory control

14. Capabilities

15. Sealing for integrity

16. Traceability of documentation

AUDIT CHECKLIST

An audit checklist should be prepared in advance of the actual audit for each element of the system that is to be audited. For each selected element, the checklist addresses the following:

1. *Name of the element to be evaluated.* An element of a calibration system is selected from the documentation referenced in an established quality plan. The selected element is predicated on the needs, expectations, and objectives of a proposed audit.

2. *Characteristics to be evaluated.* Selected metrology audit characteristics can be related to a system (policies and procedures) or to an item (instrument or product).

3. *Pertinent section and paragraph of the documented system to be evaluated.* Appropriate sections and paragraphs are selected from established policies, procedures, processes, and work instructions.

4. *Adequacy or inadequacy of the system description.* Determining the adequacy or inadequacy of a metrology system begins with the review of documented policy and procedures during an off-site "desk audit," which is followed by an on-site audit verification of predetermined elements and associated factors.

5. *Adequacy or inadequacy of systems application.* Determining the adequacy or inadequacy of a metrology system starts with the assessment of the unbiased characteristics identified during the desk audit. These characteristics are then assessed at preselected inspection and calibration stations. The results of these assessments form the basis for verifying the adequacy or inadequacy of the system.

Checklists of the major elements that comprise the system description are shown in Figures 3.1 through 3.16. The checklists shown in these figures should be implemented as required. They are implemented in addition to other factors that will impact contract quality requirements.

REPORT

A report of findings regarding the ongoing capabilities of a supplier's operations or the capabilities of a subcontractor's operation should be prepared shortly after completion of the audit. The report should include the information specified in Figure 3.17 and completed as instructed in Figure 3.18.

Requirement	References	Documentation		Application	
		Sat.	Unsat.	Sat.	Unsat.
Element: Intervals of calibration, section _____					
Characteristics:					
Basis for establishing intervals of calibration	Para. no. ____	*	*	*	*
Adequacy of recall system	Para. no. ____	*	*	*	*
Adequacy of historical records	Para. no. ____	*	*	*	*
Calibration due date	Para. no. ____	*	*	*	*
Prompt release of measuring equipment	Para. no. ____	*	*	*	*
Overdue notices	Para. no. ____	*	*	*	*
Basis for adjusting calibration intervals	Para. no. ____	*	*	*	*

Figure 3.1 Calibration system checklist for calibration intervals.

Requirement	References	Sat.	Unsat.	Sat.	Unsat.
Element: Out-of-tolerance conditions, section ___					
Characteristics:					
Definition of significant out-of-tolerance condition	Para. no. ___	*	*	*	*
Adequacy of standards	Para. no. ___	*	*	*	*
Adjustment and use prevention of equipment that does not perform satisfactorily	Para. no. ___	*	*	*	*
Adjustment of calibration levels	Para. no. ___	*	*	*	*
Notification of reporting channels of out-of-tolerance conditions	Para. no. ___	*	*	*	*

*Enter check mark if documentation and related application process is considered

Figure 3.2   Calibration system checklist for out-of-tolerance conditions.

Requirement	References	Documentation		Application	
		Sat.	Unsat.	Sat.	Unsat.
Element: Calibration system requirement, section ___					
Evaluation factors:					
Documentation of specified calibration/confirmation model	Para. no. ___	*	*	*	*
Complete documentation of prescribed calibration system	Para. no. ___	*	*	*	*
Management's commitment to the objective of calibration systems management	Para. no. ___	*	*	*	*
Management review and approval of written policy and procedures	Para. no. ___	*	*	*	*

Continued

Figure 3.3   Calibration system checklist for calibration system requirements.

Continued

Requirement	References	Documentation Sat.	Documentation Unsat.	Application Sat.	Application Unsat.
Procedures for the control of written policy and procedures	Para. no. _____	*	*	*	*
Documentation of organizational chart and responsibilities	Para. no. _____	*	*	*	*
Job description of key technical and management personnel	Para. no. _____	*	*	*	*
Documented traceability of:					
a. Product characteristic to the appropriate contract	Para. no. _____	*	*	*	*
b. Product characteristic to the associated M&TE	Para. no. _____	*	*	*	*
c. M&TE to the appropriate measurement standard (MS)	Para. no. _____	*	*	*	*
d. MS to an international or domestic standard	Para. no. _____	*	*	*	*
Provisions for the preparation or upgrading of quality plans associated with new product designs	Para. no. _____	*	*	*	*

Figure 3.3 Calibration system checklist for calibration system requirements.

Element: Adequacy of measurement standards, section _____

Evaluation factors:

Accuracy	Para. no. _____	*	*	*	*
Stability	Para. no. _____	*	*	*	*
Range	Para. no. _____	*	*	*	*
Resolution	Para. no. _____	*	*	*	*

Figure 3.4 Calibration system checklist for MS adequacy.

Element: Environment, section ____ Evaluation factors:					
Conditions that affect the accuracy and stability of M&TE and MS	Para. no. ____	*	*	*	*
Compensations and/or corrections are applied where defined environmental conditions are not met	Para. no. ____	*	*	*	*

Figure 3.5 Calibration system checklist for environmental controls.

Element: Calibration procedures, section ____ Evaluation factors:					
Method of calibration	Para. no. ____	*	*	*	*
Name of measuring instrument to be calibrated	Para. no. ____	*	*	*	*
Calibration procedure original, revision, or deletion date	Para. no. ____	*	*	*	*
Identification number of calibration procedure	Para. no. ____	*	*	*	*
Higher-level MS (primary and/or secondary)	Para. no. ____	*	*	*	*
Accuracy of MS	Para. no. ____	*	*	*	*
Environmental conditions	Para. no. ____	*	*	*	*
Application of correction factors (where appropriate)	Para. no. ____	*	*	*	*
Data (attribute and/ or variable)	Para. no. ____	*	*	*	*
Sources of calibration procedure:					
a. Standard procedures	Para. no. ____	*	*	*	*
b. Instrument manufacturer's recommended procedures	Para. no. ____	*	*	*	*

Figure 3.6 Calibration system checklist for calibration procedures. *Continued*

Continued

c. Product manufacturer's established procedures	Para. no. ____	*	*	*	*
Verification of inspection, measuring, and test procedures	Para. no. ____	*	*	*	*
Documented procedures which assure that calibrated instruments are suitably identified	Para. no. ____	*	*	*	*
Procedures for handling instruments	Para. no. ____	*	*	*	*
Procedure for the identification of M&TE and MS	Para. no. ____	*	*	*	*
Procedures for feedback data associated with out-of-tolerance M&TE and MS	Para. no. ____	*	*	*	*
Procedures for dealing with internal and external complaints	Para. no. ____	*	*	*	*
Procedures for protecting proprietary rights	Para. no. ____	*	*	*	*
Documented procedures for the performance of internal and external audits	Para. no. ____	*	*	*	*
Review and analysis of customer's requirements	Para. no. ____	*	*	*	*
Availability of complete technical data package	Para. no. ____	*	*	*	*
Financial, production, purchasing, and quality-assurance resources	Para. no. ____	*	*	*	*
Audit of established policy and procedures	Para. no. ____	*	*	*	*

Figure 3.6   Calibration system checklist for calibration procedures.

When an exit interview is conducted between members of the audit team and supplier management personnel, a copy of the minutes of the meeting should be attached to the audit summary report in Figure 3.17. The minutes of the exit interview (or conference) are usually taken by a member of the audit team. The minutes should indicate whether observed

Element: Calibration sources, section ____					
Evaluation factors:					
National Institute of Standards and Technology	Para. no. ____	*	*	*	*
Independent calibration laboratory	Para. no. ____	*	*	*	*
Instrument manufacturer	Para. no. ____	*	*	*	*
Product manufacturer	Para. no. ____	*	*	*	*
Derived from accepted values of natural physical constants	Para. no. ____	*	*	*	*
Supporting data:					
a. Certification	Para. no. ____	*	*	*	*
b. Report numbers	Para. no. ____	*	*	*	*
c. Certificate number	Para. no. ____	*	*	*	*
d. Data sheets	Para. no. ____	*	*	*	*
e. Accuracy of MS	Para. no. ____	*	*	*	*
f. Environmental conditions	Para. no. ____	*	*	*	*
g. Compliance with an appropriate system standard	Para. no. ____	*	*	*	*
h. International standard	Para. no. ____	*	*	*	*

Figure 3.7   Calibration system checklist for calibration sources.

conditions were found to be conforming or nonconforming with established policies and procedures.

When no deficiencies are observed, the responsible management personnel should be advised of conforming conditions and so noted in the minutes. If nonconforming conditions are in evidence, the observations should be clearly stated in the report. In addition, the report should clearly explain how each deficiency relates to a specific:

- Contract quality requirement
- Calibration system description
- Calibration procedure
- Work instruction

Element: Application of
records, section ____

Evaluation factors:

Instrument identification	Para. no. ____	*	*	*	*
Calibration schedules	Para. no. ____	*	*	*	*
Current calibration interval	Para. no. ____	*	*	*	*
Date of last calibration	Para. no. ____	*	*	*	*
Calibration source	Para. no. ____	*	*	*	*
Calibration procedure	Para. no. ____	*	*	*	*
Corrective action taken	Para. no. ____	*	*	*	*
Indication of operational failure	Para. no. ____	*	*	*	*
Calibration certificate of report number	Para. no. ____	*	*	*	*

Figure 3.8   Calibration system checklist for application of records.

Element: Calibration
status, section ____

Evaluation factors:

Identified throughout the production and installation process	Para. no. ____	*	*	*	*
Identification or limited-use M&TE	Para. no. ____	*	*	*	*
Tamper-proof seals affixed where appropriate	Para. no. ____	*	*	*	*

Figure 3.9   Calibration system checklist for calibration status.

Element: Control of subcontractor
calibration, section ____

Evaluation factors:

Appropriate requirements imposed on subcontractor	Para. no. ____	*	*	*	*
Audit of subcontractors	Para. no. ____	*	*	*	*

Figure 3.10   Calibration system checklist for control of subcontractor calibration.

Element: Purchaser-
supplied M&TE, section ____

Evaluation factors:

Controlled in accordance
with prescribed contract
or purchase order
requirements   Para. no. ____   *   *   *   *

Figure 3.11 Calibration system checklist for purchaser-supplied M&TE.

Element:
Storage and handling, section ____

Evaluation factors:

M&TE and MS are
protected during:

a. Storage   Para. no. ____   *   *   *   *

b. Handling   Para. no. ____   *   *   *   *

c. Transportation   Para. no. ____   *   *   *   *

Method of packaging
during storage as well
as while in use   Para. no. ____   *   *   *   *

Figure 3.12 Calibration system checklist for storage and handling.

Element: Inventory
control, section ____

Evaluation factors:

Date of inventory   Para. no. ____   *   *   *   *

Name of instrument   Para. no. ____   *   *   *   *

Accuracy of M&TE   Para. no. ____   *   *   *   *

Accuracy of MS (certified) Para. no. ____   *   *   *   *

Active/inactive instruments Para. no. ____   *   *   *   *

Figure 3.13 Calibration system checklist for inventory control.

```
Element: Capabilities,
section ____
Evaluation factors:
Internal            Para. no. ____      *     *     *     *
External            Para. no. ____      *     *     *     *
```

Figure 3.14   Calibration system checklist for capabilities.

```
Element: Sealing for
integrity, section ____
Evaluation factors:
Procedure for safeguarding
M&TE and MS:
a. Method           Para. no. ____      *     *     *     *
```

Figure 3.15   Calibration system checklist for sealing for integrity.

```
Element: Traceability
documentation and
verification, section ____
Evaluation factors:
International standards   Para. no. ____     *     *     *     *
National standards       Para. no. ____     *     *     *     *
Certificates             Para. no. ____     *     *     *     *
Reports                  Para. no. ____     *     *     *     *
Data sheets              Para. no. ____     *     *     *     *
                    *Enter check mark where documentation and
                     related application process is considered.
```

Figure 3.16   Calibration system checklist for traceability of documentation.

1. Name of facility _____

2. Location _____

3. Calibration system requirement _____

4. Inspection system/quality program requirements

5. Special contract quality requirements

6. Organizational structure

7. Names of key quality assurance personnel

8. Total number of employees _____

9. Size of facility (square feet) _____

10. Customer references (optional) _____

11. Recommendation: Approve _____ Disapprove _____

12. Provide full substantiation of recommendation

13. Surveyed by _____   14. Date _____

15. Approved by _____   16. Date _____

Figure 3.17   Calibration system audit summary report (external).

Block number	Action
1. Name of facility	Enter the name of the facility audited.
2. Location	Enter the address of the facility audited.
3. Calibration system requirement	Enter the title of the calibration system that is referenced in the purchase agreement between the customer and supplier.
4. Inspection system/quality program requirements	This requirement pertains to prime contractors and subcontractors involved in the production of an end item for which a calibration system is a specified requirement of an inspection system or quality program.
5. Special contract quality requirements	Enter as applicable.
6. Organizational structure	Obtain a copy of the company's organizational flowchart, which covers the duties of the metrology department. Attach a copy of the flowchart to the audit report. State in this block that the flowchart is attached to the report.
7. Names of key quality-assurance personnel	Enter as appropriate.
8. Total number of employees	Enter number of employees (all departments).
9. Size of facility	Enter total of square feet under roof.
10. Customer references (optional)	Enter the name(s) of facilities that have production experience with the audited facility regarding the application of the same or similar calibration system requirements.
11. Recommendation	Check approve or disapprove, as applicable.
12. Provide full substantiation of recommendation	a. Substantiate conclusions and recommendations with factual data.
	b. When applicable, identify procedures and documentation as well as instruments that are not in compliance with established calibration system requirements.
	c. Attach a copy of the audit checklist to the report.
13. Surveyed by	a. Enter the name of the person who conducted the audit.
	b. If the audit is conducted by a team, enter the team leader's name and attach a list of team participants to the report.
14. Date	Enter as appropriate.
15. Approved by	Enter the name of the quality control manager or a designated representative.
16. Date	Enter as appropriate.

Figure 3.18 Instructions for completing the audit summary report (external).

When corrective action is requested by the auditing team, action items and those responsible for them should be clearly identified. When multiple deficiencies are encountered, a milestone chart should be implemented to monitor the corrective-action process. At a minimum, the chart should:

- Specify that the audit findings be distributed within 10 working days

- List the nonconformances found

- Provide the anticipated date of correction for each deficiency

- Provide the anticipated date of the corrective report (within 30 days)

If more than 30 days are required to accomplish satisfactory corrective actions, arrangements should be made for mutually agreed upon progress reports. The progress report should be shown on a milestone schedule and supported with a cover letter.

A supplier's internal report of findings should address the information specified in the calibration audit summary report, which Figure 3.19 shows. Figure 3.20 provides instructions for preparing this report.

An audit is analogous to the "can't see the forest for the trees" syndrome because an owner of a process will *not* always *see* all of the areas that might provide opportunities for improvements. However, because of auditors' specialized training and singular focus, they are better equipped to

---

1. Department audited

2. Person(s) contacted

3. Verification stations audited

4. System elements audited

5. Calibration characteristics checked

6. Conclusions/recommendations: Conforming _____ Nonconforming _____

7. Audited by _____   8. Title _____

9. Date _____

10. Approved by _____   11. Title _____

12. Date _____

Figure 3.19   Calibration system audit summary report (internal).

Block number	Action
1. Department audited	Enter as appropriate.
2. Person(s) contacted	Enter name of department supervisor.
3. Verification stations audited	Enter inspection station(s) and/or calibration station(s) where the audit was conducted.
4. System elements audited	Enter elements of the calibration system audited. Attach a copy of the respective audit checklist to the report.
5. Calibration characteristics checked	Enter list of instrument calibration characteristics that were observed to support the audit report.
6. Conclusions/ recommendations	Substantiate conclusions and recommendations with factual data. Identify processes and documentation that are not in compliance with established calibration system requirements.
7. Audited by	Enter name(s) of person(s) that conducted the audit.
8. Title	Enter as appropriate.
9. Date	Enter as appropriate.
10. Approved by	Enter name of responsible management supervisor.
11. Title	Enter as appropriate.
12. Date	Enter as appropriate.

Figure 3.20   Instructions for preparing the calibration system audit summary report (internal).

make recommendations for improvements in established policies, processes, and procedures to management personnel where appropriate.

When conducting a metrology audit, caution must be taken to select only those elements of a calibration system and their related factors that can be traceable to active documents. These active documents include policy, procedures, and processes. Where applicable, selected characteristics should be traceable to a specific contract or purchase order. This method of conducting an audit will confirm to both internal and external customers that the supplier of metrology services is (or is not) complying with the written quality plan and that the associated policies, procedures, and processes are (or are not) accomplishing their intended purpose for controlling specified quality requirements.

ENDNOTE

1. ISO 10012:2003, *Measurement management systems—Requirements for measurement processes and measuring equipment,* clause 5.1.

4

Case Study 1—Supplier with Unknown Calibration System Capabilities

T he customer's primary goal is that the causes of inadequate production processes are immediately identified and corrected so that product quality is maintained and delivery schedules are met. The supplier is concerned about the problems in production processes that lead to added quality costs and delay in delivery schedules. The supplier also fears possible loss of repeat business caused by inadvertently delivering nonconforming products to the customer.

This case study can be used in two ways. Obviously, it demonstrates how proper preparation makes a products' sale, production, and delivery easier for both the supplier and customer. But perhaps, more importantly, the case study shows the prime contractor how to examine the quality and calibration systems of its suppliers. The case study encourages the use of the audit to improve capability in cases in which the initial review might find elements of inadequate compliance.

This case study also shows the negative impact that errors of omission (as described in chapter 1) have on a proposed supplier when the supplier cannot provide satisfactory evidence of its QA capabilities during the customer's pre-award survey. *Pre-award survey* means "an evaluation by a surveying activity of a prospective contractor's [supplier] capability to perform a proposed contract."[1] This survey is conducted by a team consisting of financial, production, and QA representatives. Occasionally, a safety specialist is added to the team when conditions warrant. However, this text is focused only on the functions of QA personnel.*

---

* Most pre-award surveys that are performed at a proposed supplier's facility pertain to the inspection system or a quality program's capabilities. However, this book is focused on the calibration system, which is a part of a specified inspection system or quality program.

The pre-award survey supports the belief that requesting the lowest bidder is only the first step in the solicitation process. The customer must also assure that potential suppliers are responsible and have the capability to meet the technical requirements of a solicitation (proposed contract). The customer places heavy reliance on the technology and capabilities of its suppliers. This reliance must be established or maintained prior to issuing a contract award in which a potential supplier's capability is unknown. The reliance is maintained on an ongoing basis when a supplier's capabilities provide assurance that products and services offered are in accordance with a prescribed requirement.

There are several factors that a supplier must address when establishing evidence of its own capabilities. In addition to having financial and production resources or the ability to obtain them within the time constraints required by the customer, a supplier must:

- Be able to comply with a specified performance and delivery schedule

- Have a satisfactory performance record regarding the production of identical or similar items solicited

- Have required measuring equipment of known accuracy

- Have the ability to obtain additional resources as required

Customers try to preclude the possibility of awarding a contract to an apparent low bidder with unknown capabilities. Experienced purchasers generally add a provision to their solicitation that will permit a QA representative to conduct an in-plant audit to assure that the proposed supplier has an acceptable calibration system in place. The customer wants to be assured that the system is current and, when necessary, will be upgraded appropriately.

The fact that all of the required calibration documentation is not readily available to an auditor does not necessarily mean that work will not be awarded. The customer may examine all of the facts associated with the solicited statement of work. This is particularly apparent when a low bidder indicates that its company has extensive experience in the production of similar items. An in-depth analysis of existing documentation and discussions between the auditor and key supplier personnel will enhance the decision process that will ultimately be in the best interest of both supplier and low bidder. For example, a decision to recommend an affirmative or negative contract award without addressing all of the elements of the system and associated factors that impact a specified calibration system can lead to errors of omission. When the results of an audit indicate that a supplier has a satisfactory performance record and that acceptable policies and procedures are in place, it reduces the risk of producing a product with measuring instruments of questionable accuracy.

When evidence of a supplier's QA capabilities is unavailable at the time of the survey but the auditors determine that the supplier understands the proposed contract quality requirements, the supplier may offset negative factors and support its case with satisfactory planning. Under this condition, the survey team may consider the supplier's request for the contract award to the purchaser after satisfactory documented planning is made available. If the survey team decides that a proposed supplier's planning is inadequate, the team will have no other recourse but to submit a "no award" recommendation to the purchaser.

The following factors support an effective plan for remediation:

1. *Identifying the proposed contract quality requirements on a milestone chart or another acceptable medium.* Milestone planning is a process by which the QA personnel implement and maintain metrology requirements through a comprehensive quality plan. The primary purpose of milestone planning is to ensure and make evident that the specified requirements of a metrology system meet both internal and external customers' needs and expectations in a timely manner.

2. *Making arrangements for the acquisition of the required inspection equipment, M&TE, and MSs.* The proposed supplier seeks those companies that have the required elements in place. The supplier must act with the same diligence that its customer employs.

3. *Determining the requirements and the availability of additional QA personnel.* The acquisition of additional QA personnel can offset deficiencies, if cost-efficient. When specific skills are unavailable within the organization, they can be acquired from an independent calibration laboratory or from a qualified consultant.

4. *Identifying the availability and capability of outside calibration sources.* The availability of outside calibration sources is normally identified from a list of approved calibration sources or from an ANSI/ISO/ASQ Q9000 list of certified and registered companies. When a proposed source of calibration is not referenced on any of these lists, the prime contractor must verify a proposed supplier's calibration capability before awarding a purchase order to a subcontractor.

When the four factors are addressed, the supplier who initially did not have a calibration system in place at the time of the pre-award survey may compete for business and produce effectively. A supplier who is able to plan and act on this remediate plan often proves to be an acceptable supplier of products and services. With a minimum amount of guidance and an opportunity to prove its capability, the supplier will not only produce acceptable products but also support methods for controlling product quality.

When a proposed supplier reflects a clear understanding of the technical requirements of a solicitation, it eliminates the impression that its capabilities are inadequate (see Figures 4.1 and 4.2). In this case study, the proposed contractor's policies and procedures and calibration documentation are insufficient to adequately determine its QA capabilities. Under the present conditions, the calibration system does not cover the QA requirements of the solicitation.

From: Contract administrator

To: Quality control manager

1. Technical data requirements:

    a. Part name: valve, hydraulic service

    b. Quantity: 100 each

    c. Assembly drawing number: XXX456-1X

    d. Inspection system requirements: MIL-I-45208A

    e. Calibration system requirements: MIL-STD 45662A

2. Performance requirements:

    a. No leaks will be permitted when the valve is subjected to a hydrostatic test pressure of 6000 psig with the valve in the open position.

    b. Any weeping, porosity, or permanent deformation shall be cause for rejection.

3. Product inspection site: point of production

4. Product acceptance point: point of production

5. F.O.B. point: destination

6. Attachments:

    a. Assembly drawing

    b. Component drawings

7. Customer: U.S. government

8. Delivery schedule: 180 days (by 7/3/0X)

Figure 4.1 Abstract of solicitation requirements.

Contractor: John Doe Corporation

Purpose: To determine subject contractor's capabilities regarding the application of MIL-STD-45662A calibration system requirements

Persons contacted:

a. President

b. Quality control manager

Supplier's quality assurance structure:

Position	Years of experience
Quality control manager	18
Inspection supervisor	12
Calibration technician	9
Four product inspectors	Average 11 years

Types of products produced:

Mechanical components and assemblies with product tolerances of from 0.001–0.0001 inch.

Size of plant:

a. Size of tract: 4000 square feet

b. Area under roof: 3200 square feet

c. Number of buildings: one

d. Kind of structure: cinder block

Calibration facilities and equipment:

a. Calibration room: 225 square feet

b. Measurement standards: precision gage blocks

c. M&TE: a sufficient amount to satisfy solicitation requirements

Observations:

a. The proposed contractor maintains an informal calibration system and relies on verbal orders to accomplish many of the functions of the calibration process.

b. The calibration technician is wholly responsible for performing instrument calibration. No written instructions are furnished for this purpose.

c. Calibration documentation is limited to the application of calibration labels to the respective instruments.

Figure 4.2 Pre-award survey report.

The conditions previously mentioned were brought to the attention of the company's president and QC manager at a meeting held in the company's conference room. The president recognized the shortcomings and stated that this was his first experience with the application of calibration systems management. He said that the QC manager made him aware of what was needed to upgrade the required policies and procedures.

The company president advised that additional personnel and outside assistance would be acquired to prepare for and upgrade pertinent policies, procedures, and documentation within the time constraints of the solicitation. The president's comments were supported with a schedule of anticipated completion dates (see Figure 4.3). However, a decision regarding the proposed supplier's ability to meet the solicitation requirements was held in abeyance pending the examination of three instruments that were previously calibrated by the proposed supplier. This was accomplished by checking the adequacy of condions within the calibration area as well as checking three instruments: a zero to 2000 pounds-per-square-inch gage (psig) pressure gage, a one-inch micrometer, and a 12-inch vernier caliper.

Topic		Scheduled Completion Dates
1. Planning	***	1/14/0X
2. Personnel	***	1/14/0X
3. Inspection equipment	***	1/14/0X
4. Calibration sources	***	1/14/0X
5 Written calibration description	• •	
a. Responsibilities	***	2/7/0X
b. System maintenance	***	2/7/0X
c. Calibration intervals	***	2/7/0X
d. Traceability of measurement standards	***	2/7/0X
e. Environmental controls	***	2/7/0X
f. Calibration status	***	2/14/0X
g. Objective evidence		2/14/0X
h. Calibration audits		3/14/0X
Legend: *** = Ongoing process		

Figure 4.3 Milestone chart calibration system requirements.

CALIBRATION AREA ASSESSMENT

An inspection of the calibration area revealed the following:

- The calibration area was clean and free from extraneous items.

- The room temperature in the calibration area was stabilized at 68° F.

- Instruments were properly protected in containers. When not in use, they were stored safely in cabinets.

- The surface plates on which calibrations were made were found to be calibrated by an independent calibration laboratory. The plates were free from nicks, cracks, and extraneous items.

- Reference standards were calibrated by an independent laboratory.

- Calibrations provided by an independent laboratory were supported with a certified report. The report included quality data showing the results of measurements made, applicable calibration system adopted, and satisfactory evidence of traceability of the laboratory standards by an unbroken chain of calibration events to NIST. The report was signed by an official of the organization responsible for providing the calibration service.

PRESSURE GAGE ASSESSMENT

During the assessment of the pressure gage, the following supporting information was identified:

- Identification number: PR-101

- Instrument accuracy: +/− 10 psig

- Instrument range: 0–2000 psig

- Usage: up to 600 psig

- Company's reference standard: pressure gage with a 10:1 accuracy ratio

The company's reference (transfer) standard, which was used to calibrate its working pressure gage, was calibrated by an independent laboratory with the use of a deadweight tester. This tester, whose accuracy is traceable to NIST, had an accuracy of +/− 0.1 percent of output pressure.

The working pressure gage and the reference standard were examined for physical damage prior to integrating them into the test stand. It was noted that with no pressure on the gage, the indicating needle was not located directly over the zero reading. This was immediately rectified by accessing an adjustment device located on the gage and adjusting the indicator directly over the zero.

It is important to note that, although the inspection pressure gage was capable of testing pressures up to 2000 psig, the maximum pressure test required by the product specification was 600 psig. Therefore, this fact was taken into consideration when selecting pressure values for verification of the instrument's adequacy as well as the associated policy and procedures. The selected pressure valves and auditor's findings were as follows:

Characteristics Examined	Supplier's Observations	Auditor's Findings*
100 psig	105 psig	105 psig
200 psig	205 psig	205 psig
300 psig	305 psig	305 psig
400 psig	405 psig	405 psig
500 psig	505 psig	505 psig
600 psig	605 psig	605 psig

* Compensating correction factor of 5 psig was added to the calibration status tag to accommodate departures from the nominal values shown under the first column. This status tag is conspicuously attached to the working gage and in full view of the calibration and testing technician.

ONE-INCH MICROMETER ASSESSMENT

During the asessment of the one-inch micrometer, the following supporting information was identified:

- Identification number: MI-201

- Discrimination: 0.0001 inch

- Instrument Accuracy: +/– 0.0001 inch

- Instrument range: 0–1.000 inch

- Usage: full range

- Company's reference standards:

  - Set of 81 precision gage blocks (style 1—rectangle) with a tolerance of + 8 and – 5 microinches

  - Precision measuring ball (size 0.12500 inch) with an accuracy of 0.0002 inch

The company's metrology specialist checked the one-inch micrometer using precision gage blocks with values of 0.100-, 0.200-, 0.450-, 0.750-, and 0.950-inch as standards. The instrument was examined for physical and mechanical damage and subsequently checked in an area that was dust- and particle-free and on instrument-measuring surfaces that were cleaned with a dust-free cloth. Verification of the supplier's observation was accomplished subsequent to verifying the flatness of the micrometer anvil. The micrometer anvil was checked for flatness at four quadrants with a 0.12500-inch precision ball and was found to be acceptable. The auditor concurred with the conclusions made by the supplier's calibration technician, as the following data shows.

Characteristics Examined	Supplier's Observation*	Auditor's Findings
0.1000 inch	0.0999 inch	0.1000 inch
0.2000 inch	0.1999 inch	0.2000 inch
0.4500 inch	0.4499 inch	0.4500 inch
0.7500 inch	0.7499 inch	0.7500 inch
0.9500 inch	0.9499 inch	0.9500 inch

*   Records indicate that the variations from the instruments nominal size as shown in column two above were rectified by proper adjustments to the instruments. Since the tightest product tolerance associated with products produced is less than 0.001 of an inch, these variations do not have a negative impact on the acceptance or rejection of related product characteristics. However the supplier did indicate that this condition was directed to the attention of its material review board for review, concurrence, and to determine its impact on the adequacy of established calibration internals.

VERNIER CALIPER ASSESSMENT

During the assessment of the vernier caliper, the following supporting information was identified:

- Identification number: MI-301

- Discrimination: 0.001 inch

- Instrument accuracy: +/– 0.001 inch

- Instrument range: 0–12.000 inches

- Company's reference standards:

  - Precision gage blocks

  - Precision measuring rods

All assessments were made on calibration characteristics that were previously checked by the company's metrology specialist with measuring standards of known accuracy. The instruments were calibrated within an established calibration interval with standards traceable to NIST. The vernier caliper blade (measuring surface for external measurements) was examined for wear with a precision roll and found to be acceptable prior to making the following observations:

Characteristic Examined	Standard Used	Supplier's Observations	Auditor's Findings
2.500 inch	Gage block	2.500 inch	2.500 inch
4.000 inch	Gage block	4.000 inch	4.000 inch
6.500 inch	Precision rod	6.500 inch	6.500 inch
8.000 inch	Precision rod	8.000 inch	8.000 inch
10.500 inch	Precision rod	10.500 inch	10.500 inch
12.00 inch	Precision rod	12.000 inch	12.500 inch

The audit report was submitted to the buying function. A recommendation for a contract award regarding calibration capabilities was accepted.

CONCLUSION

Today more and more suppliers recognize that the establishment and maintenance of a calibration system is imperative for verifying that products are produced right the first time. However, many suppliers fall short of documenting a satisfactory calibration system. This can be attributed to several causes, including:

- Some suppliers are simply unfamiliar with or are not aware of the calibration system standards and associated handbooks that are available to them from ANSI, ASQ, and ISO.

- Other suppliers are aware of these standards but elect to adopt only a portion or none of the applicable elements of an appropriate calibration system. In addition, improvements of deficiencies in the calibration system are normally made only after the receipt of deficiencies in the system that are detected and reported by internal or external customers.

- Some offerers of products and services who have been in business for an extended period of time who are financially stable and are not motivated by any of its internal or external customers to establish and maintain an appropriate calibration system.

The American Society for Quality, the American National Standards Institute, and the International Organization for Standardization and their memberships have made large contributions towards improving quality systems management nationally and internationally. For example, over the past two decades these organizations, with dedicated support from their memberships, have published quality-related textbooks, standards, and technical papers. Its members regularly conduct seminars, conferences, and training programs for its members as well as for the public in general. Last but not least, its ANSI/ISO/ASQ Q9000 certification program has brought and continues to bring new offerers of products and services under its umbrella of registered and certified suppliers.

ENDNOTE

1. U.S. Department of Defense, General Services Administration, and National Aeronautics and Space Administration, *Federal Acquisition Regulation,* part 9, clause 9.101 (1995).

5

Communicating Calibration Capabilities: Using Effective Documentation

This chapter provides examples of QA data that are crucial in verifying the adequacy of an acceptable calibration system as well as for providing an indication of a supplier's calibration capabilities. The chapter includes sample documents in a case study format that demonstrate the use of documentation to monitor compliance with a calibration system requirement.

ABSTRACT OF CONTRACT QUALITY REQUIREMENT

One of the most critical elements of a metrology system is the timely receipt of an all-inclusive abstract of contract quality requirements (see Figure 5.1). This abstract must clearly describe the work and provide the assurance that applicable drawings, specifications, and standards are on hand or readily available when needed. Each abstract or equivalent method of summarizing contract quality requirements should be reviewed in depth to ensure that technical requirements are understood by the metrology manager and the manager's staff of specialists. This review is particularly important for new or different product designs. In addition, new-product design requirements should be compared with previously prepared quality plans. When a new product design has a direct impact on the metrology portion of a quality plan, these new requirements must be compared with previously prepared procedures and processes and tailored accordingly to meet the new requirements.

From: Contract administrator

To: Quality control manager

Subject: Contract quality requirements

1. Technical data

   a. Part name: shaft

   b. Quantity: 500 each

   c. Drawing (part number): ABC-123

   d. Inspection system requirements: ANSI/ISO/ASQC Q9002

   e. Calibration system requirements: ISO-10012-1

   f. Product inspection site: place of production

   g. Product acceptance site: place of production

   h. Delivery schedule: 180 days (by 7/3/0X)

   i. F.O.B. point: Destination

2. Attachments

   a. Drawing number: ABC-123

3. Customer

   a. U.S. Government
      Naval Supply Center
      Norfolk, VA 23515

4. Comments: Specifications ANSI/ISO/ASQC Q9002 referenced in the abstract was furnished to the quality control department under a previous abstract of contract quality requirements.

Figure 5.1   Abstract of contract quality requirement.

Communication of contract quality requirements between the supplier's designated contract administrator and the manager of the metrology department (via the QA director) must be accomplished as early as possible so that:

- Differences of opinions, ambiguity, or omissions can be rectified without jeopardizing an established delivery schedule.

- The metrology department will have sufficient lead time to review the complete technical package so that satisfactory planning can be accomplished correctly the first time.

- The need for additional personnel, plant facilities, inspection equipment, and M&TE can be determined.

- The adequacy of existing policy, procedures, and processes can be identified.

- Where appropriate, the capabilities of potential independent calibration laboratories, or subcontractors can be identified.

Calibration records are essential for providing internal and external customers with an indication of a metrology department's ability to meet new calibration system requirements. They document the ability to maintain established policies, procedures, and processes. In addition, records provide an indication of instrument stability and reliability. A history of objective quality data forms the basis for the establishment or adjustment of calibration intervals. Records must be held in a format that is readily available for use by management and operations personnel.

MASTER REQUIREMENTS LIST

From the abstract, the metrology manager or a designated representative will prepare a master requirements list (see Figure 5.2). The master requirements list is an important *component* of a supplier's overall quality plan. This list is provided to the metrology department for planning and implementation purposes. The list identifies product characteristics associated with a particular product design as well as the measuring instruments that are used to inspect the respective product characteristics. This list provides support to the quality data that is entered in the appropriate calibration and product observation records. The master requirements list, in conjunction with an applicable product observation record (which also addresses an applicable purchase order or contract number) and a calibration record, completes the traceability loop. This list simplifies the investigation of customer complaints and becomes the initial focus for the investigation of justified customer complaints.

CALIBRATION EQUIPMENT LIST

Following the review of technical documents associated with a specific contract, the metrology manager, in concert with the QC manager, prepares a list of MSs and working instruments that are required for all metrology

Product Characteristic Code Number	Characteristic Identification	Measuring Device (MD)	MD Identification Number	MD Code Number
101	1.500" + 0.000" – 0.001"	1"–2" Micrometer, outside	C10001	MD1
102	1.000" + 0.000" – 0.001"	1" Micrometer, outside*	C10002	MD2
103	True position	Dial indicator	C10003	MD3
104	0.375 + 0.001" – 0.000"	"Go/no go" plug gage	C10004	MD4
201	2.000" +/– 0.005"	0"–6" Vernier caliper	C10005	MD5
202	0.750" +/– 0.005"	0"–6" Vernier caliper	C10006	MD6
203	2.750 +/– 0.005"	0"–6" Vernier caliper	C10007	MD7

Prepared by _____ Date _____

* For this characteristic, when the inspection process indicates that the manufactured product is larger than one inch, use a 1"–2" micrometer to obtain the indicated measurement.

Figure 5.2 Master requirements list, number one, drawing ABC-123.

operations. This list includes all instruments used to make required measurements or used to calibrate, regardless of ownership (see Figure 5.3). By establishing and maintaining inventory lists of both active and inactive inspection equipment and M&TE, QA personnel are able to prepare a master quality plan for each new product design. The calibration equipment list also supports the individual planning and application of individual calibration technicians.

The active and inactive calibration equipment lists provide management and operations personnel with ready access to information that is critical to the:

- Availability of inspection, measuring and test equipment that might or might not be required by a new product design

Name of Instrument	Nominal Size	Accuracy Value	Quantity	Application
Precision gage block set	*	*	1 set	**
Micrometer, outside	0"–1"	+/–0.0001"	1 each	***
Micrometer, outside	0"–2"	+/–0.0001"	1 each	***
Dial indicator	0"–0.005"	+/–0.0001"	1 each	***
"Go/no go" plug gage	0.375"	+/–0.0001"	1 each	***
Vernier caliper	0"–6"	+/–0.001"	1 each	***

*Refer to certificate of calibration located in the respective gage block set container
**Measurement standard
***Product inspection

Figure 5.3   Calibration equipment list.

- Need for inactive instruments to be calibrated and transferred to the active list of calibrated M&TE

- Assessment of whether instruments in current inventory have the accuracies required by the new product design

- Assessment of the need to upgrade existing calibration procedures

- Assessement of the need to establish new calibration procedures

The following factors should be addressed when preparing an instrument inventory list:

1. Instrument nomenclature

2. Number of identical instruments

3. Product manufacturer's instrument identification number

4. Instrument manufacturer's instrument identification number

5. Instrument discrimination

6. Instrument accuracy

7. Description of use

CALIBRATION PROCEDURES FOR M&TE

The primary purpose of preparing calibration procedures is to provide metrology personnel with a detailed description of how to perform calibrations of each inspection, measuring, and testing device that is used within the system. The procedures identify the standards that will be used to verify the accuracy of the calibrated working instruments. In addition to providing a step-by-step calibration procedure, calibration instructions should address:

- The accuracy tolerance of the calibrated instrument

- The area of uncertainty of the MS as well as the area of uncertainty of the characteristic being calibrated

- The accuracy ratio between the MS and the characteristic being calibrated

Calibration procedures are required for the measuring devices referenced on the master requirements list. For example, Figures 5.4 through 5.8 show the calibration procedures for the measuring devices in the master requirements list in Figure 5.2.

PRODUCT OBSERVATION RECORDS FOR M&TE

The observation record of product inspection (see Figure 5.9) contains the following additional factors that pertain to the product and instrument traceability loop:

1. *Master requirements list code number.* This number identifies the appropriate number that can be traceable to a specific master requirements list assigned to a specific product.

2. *Product characteristic code number.* This number identifies the product characteristic in question, which is listed on the master requirements list.

3. *Measurement device code number.* This number identifies the specific measuring device that was used to check the particular product characteristic in question.

Instrument nomenclature: Micrometer, outside, 1"–2"
Identification number: C10001
Calibration procedure number: CP-1
Instrument accuracy: +/– 0.0001"
Discrimination: 0.0001"
Range of instrument: 1"–2"
Measurement standard required: precision gage block set
Accuracy of measurement standard: refer to certified calibration record
    for accuracy values

Calibration process:

- The instrument shall be calibrated in a room having a temperature between 65° F and 75° F, +/– 5° F. The temperature shall be stabilized and shall remain constant during the calibration process. The room must be dust- and particle-free during the calibration process.

- Visually examine the instrument for damage prior to calibration.

- Clean the instrument's measuring surfaces with a lint-free cloth prior to the start of calibration.

- Check the micrometer over gage blocks 1.000", 1.250", 1.750", and 2.000".

- When measured readings exceed the accuracy tolerance of the micrometer measurement, remove the instrument from service for adjustment and recalibration.

- Document calibration results on the calibration form.

- Out-of-tolerance conditions should be documented on the metrology deficiency report form and brought to the attention of the quality control manager for necessary action.

- Attach a calibration status label to the instrument and its container.

Prepared by _____ Date _____

Approved by _____ Date _____

Figure 5.4 Calibration procedure for micrometer, 1–2 inches.

Other pertinent information in the observation record of product inspection that must be considered when accessing traceability information are the actual measurements. Those measurements should be compared with the values referenced in a customer complaint and the purchase order or contract, as appropriate.

Instrument nomenclature: Micrometer, outside, 0"–1"
Identification number: C10002
Calibration procedure number: CP-2
Instrument accuracy: +/– 0.0001"
Discrimination: 0.0001"
Range: 0"–1"
Measurement standard required:

   a. Precision gage block set
      Accuracy of measurement standard: refer to certified calibration
      record for accuracy values

   b. Precision measuring ball: 12500"
      Accuracy: 0.0002"

Calibration process:

- The instrument must be calibrated in a room having a temperature between 65° F and 75° F that should remain constant during the calibration process.

- The calibration area must be dust- and particle-free during the calibration process.

- Visually examine the instrument for damage before calibration.

- Clean the instrument's measuring surface with a lint-free cloth prior to the start of calibration.

- Check the micrometer anvil (measuring surface) with a 0.125" precision measuring ball for flatness at four quadrants. Remove the micrometer from service for repair, recalibration, or replacement when the flatness exceeds 0.0002".

- Take measurements on the instrument at five places over precision gage blocks 0.100", 0.375", 0.500", 0.750", and 1.000". When measured readings exceed the accuracy tolerance of the micrometer measurements, remove the instrument from service for adjustment and/or repair.

- Document calibration results on the calibration form.

- Document out-of-tolerance conditions on the metrology deficiency report form and bring to the attention of the quality control manager.

- Attach a calibration status label to the instrument and its container.

Prepared by _____ Date _____

Approved by _____ Date _____

Figure 5.5   Calibration procedure for micrometer, 0–1 inch.

Instrument nomenclature: Dial indicator
Identification number: C10003
Calibration procedure number: CP-3
Instrument accuracy: +/– 0.0001"
Discrimination: 0.0001"
Range of instrument: 0"–0.005"
Measurement standard required: precision gage block set
Accuracy of measurement standard: refer to certified calibration record
    for accuracy values

Calibration process:

- The instrument should be calibrated in a room having a temperature between 65° F and 75° F that must remain constant during the calibration process.

- The calibration area must be dust- and particle-free during the calibration process.

- Visually examine the instrument for damage before calibrating the instrument and verify that the shaft that initiates the dial movement moves freely. If the shaft does not move freely, remove the dial indicator from service for repair and/or replacement.

- Clean all measuring surfaces with a lint-free cloth before the start of calibration.

- Required equipment:
  a. Surface plate
  b. Parallel bar
  c. Precision gage block set
  d. Height gage mounting fixture

- Proceed as follows:
  a. Zero the dial indicator over a 0.100″ gage block.
  b. Take measurements over gage blocks 0.101″, 0.102″, 0.103″, 0.104″, and 0.105″.

- When measured value exceeds the specified accuracy of the dial indicator, remove the instrument from service for repair, recalibration, or replacement.

- Document calibration results on the calibration form.

- Out-of-tolerance conditions should be documented on the metrology deficiency report form and brought to the attention of the quality control manager for necessary action.

- Attach a calibration status label to the instrument and its container.

Prepared by _____ Date _____

Approved by _____ Date _____

Figure 5.6   Calibration procedure for dial indicator.

Instrument nomenclature: "Go/no go" plug gage

Identification number: C10004

Calibration procedure number: CP-4

Accuracy of plug gage: 0.0002"

Measurement standards required:

   a. Precision gage block set

   b. Bench micrometer with 0.000050" discrimination

Calibration process:

- The gage shall be calibrated in a room having a temperature between 65° F and 75° F, +/– 5° F. The temperature must be stabilized and remain constant during the calibration process.

- The room must be dust- and particle-free during the calibration process.

- Visually examine the instrument for damage prior to calibration.

- Clean the instrument's measuring surfaces with a lint-free cloth prior to the start of calibration.

- Place the bench micrometer on a surface plate and set it up with a gage block that represents the size of the plug that is being calibrated.

- Measure the "go" member of the gage as well as the "no go" member at six locations, front, middle, and back, taking three readings at 0° and three readings at 90°.

- When the measured value exceeds the specified accuracy requirements, the plug will be removed from service and either returned to the instrument manufacturer for rework to specified accuracy requirements or scrapped.

- Document calibration results on the calibration form.

- Out-of-tolerance conditions should be documented on the metrology deficiency report form and brought to the attention of the quality control manager for necessary action.

- Attach a calibration status label to the instrument as well as to the instrument's container.

Prepared by _____ Date _____

Approved by _____ Date _____

Figure 5.7 Calibration procedure for "go/no go" plug gage.

Instrument nomenclature: Vernier caliper
Identification number: C10005
Calibration procedure number: CP-5
Instrument accuracy: +/– 0.0001"
Discrimination: 0.0001"
Range: 0"–6"
Measurement standard required: precision gage block set

Calibration process:

- The instrument shall be calibrated in a room having a temperature between 65° F and 75° F, +/– 5° F. The temperature shall be stabilized and shall remain constant during the calibration process.

- The room must be dust-free during the calibration process.

- Visually examine the instrument for damage prior to calibration.

- Clean the instrument's measuring surface with a lint-free cloth prior to the start of calibration.

- Check the vernier's wear jaw by visual means and by taking measurements over a gage pin or ring gage at the front, middle, and back side of the wear jaw.

- Check measurements on the vernier caliper over gage block sizes 0.500", 0.750", 2.000", 4.000", and 6.000".

- Document calibration results on the calibration form provided for this purpose.

- Out-of-tolerance conditions shall be documented on the metrology deficiency report form and brought to the attention of the quality control manager for necessary action.

- Attach a calibration status label to the instrument as well as to its container.

Prepared by _____ Date _____

Approved by _____ Date _____

Figure 5.8   Calibration procedure for vernier caliper.

Observation Record

Item description Shaft

Spec. no. N/A

Dwg. no. ABC-123

Other —

Characteristic and Measuring Device Code Number

Insp. station	Purchase order or contract number	Sampling plan: ANSI/ASQ Z1.4 N-II-S	Julian date	Revision no.	Lot size	Sample size	Accept no.	Reject no.	M/req. list no.	101 (MD1)	102 (MD2)	103 (MD3)	104 (MD4)	201 (MD5)	202 (MD5)	203 (MD5)	No. obs.	No. def. obs.	% Defective	Disposition	Inspector
5	123xxxxx	Major 1.5	66	–	500	50	2	3	1	50/0	50/0	50/4	50/0	–/–	–/–	–/–	200	4	2	R	SI
5	123xxxxx	Minor 4.0	66	–	–	–	7	8	1	–/–	–/–	–/–	–/–	50/0	50/0	50/0	150	0	0	A	SI
11	123xxxxx	Resubmitted								50/0	50/0	50/0	50/0				200	0	0	A	SI
11	123xxxxx	Lot												50/0	50/0	50/0	150	0	0	A	SI

1: SPC program   2: Receiving inspection   3: First article inspection   4: In-process inspection   5: Final inspection   6: Shipping inspection

Figure 5.9   Sample observation record of product inspection.

METROLOGY DEFICIENCY REPORT

The calibration technicians should report significant out-of-tolerance conditions to the metrology manager and, when appropriate, to other department managers, depending on the M&TE used and that equipment's known accuracy. This report alerts the metrology manager to the problem so that he or she can take immediate corrective action to preclude any further acceptance of products tested with equipment whose accuracy is in question.

NONCONFORMING PRODUCT REPORT

The nonconforming product report is issued to preclude the repetitive acceptance of nonconforming product and services. This report helps determine whether a complaint is related to any instruments whose accuracy might be in question, identify the assignable cause, and ensure satisfactory corrective action.

EVIDENCE OF CAPABILITY

The process of establishing objective quality evidence regarding calibration capability that will meet the interests of a product manufacturer or an independent calibration laboratory as well as meet the expectations of customers starts with contract quality requirements that are clearly communicated from the purchaser to the supplier of a product or service and from the supplier to the metrology department. Clearly communicated contract quality requirements beget a robust quality plan. A product's required measuring instruments are identified from the quality plan, the abstract of contract quality, or a combination thereof (see Figures 5.1 and 5.10).

USING THE SAMPLE DOCUMENTS

An observation record of product inspection (see Figure 5.9) is included in this chapter for the purpose of establishing a process for tracing a defective product characteristic to the specific measuring device that was used to check a defective product characteristic. This operation is one of the important steps that are required in the corrective-action process.

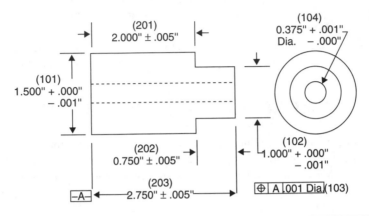

Part name: Shaft
Part number: ABC-123
Characteristic codes:
          Major: 101–104
          Minor: 201–203

Figure 5.10   Abstract of solicitation requirements.

The first step in the traceability process is to identify the master requirements list (Figure 5.2) that pertains to the product characteristic in question. This information can be found in the observation record of product inspection. The master requirements list number is in the 10th column. The master requirements list will provide the necessary information to satisfactorily investigate the cause, which is crucial to preclude the recurrence of the reported deficiency.

If the deficiency is found to be related to the measuring device, then focus will be centered on correcting the out-of-tolerance condition of the respective measuring device. If the pertinent measuring instrument is found to be in tolerance, then the investigation will be directed to the processes that were used to produce the product.

The metrology deficiency report is used for reporting out-of-tolerance conditions. The information contained in the sample report in Figure 5.11 is associated with the 2-11-0X entry shown under "Work Performance" in the calibration record, Figure 5.12. Investigation results regarding the inadequacy of the processes that were used to manufacture the product are documented in the nonconforming material report, Figure 5.13.

To: Metrology manager

From: Calibration technician

Report number: 1

Date: 2/11/0X

Measuring device: Micrometer, outside, one inch

Instrument identification number: C100002

Calibration procedure number: CP-2

Reply due date: 2/18/0X

Signature of requestor: S/J. McTechnician

Out-of-tolerance condition: Measured values for characteristic 0.001"–1.000" have drifted from their nominal size by 0.00005". While this is still an in-tolerance condition, it indicates a trend toward an out-of-tolerance condition.

Corrective action reply as to cause: Normal wear trend

Recommended action: Continue to calibrate weekly and do not proceed to a revised calibration frequency until the conditions of the calibration system manual are met.

Investigator's signature: S/J. McMetrology

Title: Metrology manager

Date: 2/15/0X

Figure 5.11   Metrology deficiency report.

Metrology managers who establish a uniform policy, assign responsibilities, and provide their team of calibration technicians with robust procedures and processes will experience little or no difficulty in convincing second- or third-party quality assessors that they have administrative and technical capabilities. When providers of products and services demonstrate that they have both administrative and technical capabilities, they provide assurance to internal and external managers that the probability of product rejections, production delays, late deliveries of product and services, customer complaints, and losses will be minimal.

Calibration Record

Instrument _Micrometer, outside, one inch_

Model _N/A_   Location _Final inspection_

I.D. no. _C10002_   Accuracy _+/– 0.0001"_

Procedure no. _CP–2_   Discrimination _0.0001"_

Calibration freq. _P*_   Tamper-proof ☐ Yes ☒ No

Other _*Prior to use_

Date calibrated	Due date	Calibration technician	.001"	.375"	.500"	.750"	1.000"	Anvil	Vis.			
1/10/0x	P	*JM*	.001	.375	.500	.750	1.000	OK	OK			
1/11/0x	P	*JM*	.001	.375	.500	.750	1.000	OK	OK			
1/12/0x	P	*JM*	.001	.375	.500	.750	1.000	OK	OK			
1/13/0x	P	*JM*	.001	.375	.500	.750	1.000	OK	OK			
1/14/0x	Change freq. to weekly		–	–	–	–	–	–	–			
1/21/0x	1/28/0x	*JM*	.001	.375	.500	.750	1.000	OK	OK			
1/28/0x	2/4/0x	*JM*	.001	.375	.500	.750	1.000	OK	OK			
2/4/0x	2/11/0x	*JM*	.001	.375	.500	.750	1.000	OK	OK			
2/11/0x	2/18/0x	*JM*	.09995	.37495	.49995	.74995	.99995	OK	OK			

Work performance — Characteristic identification — Measured value

Figure 5.12   Sample calibration record of M&TE.

Distribution: _____   Report number _____

Quality control manager ___ Engineering ___ Plant manager ___

With production lot _____ Other _____

Part name: Shaft   Part number: ABC-123   Job number: JN-100

Sampling plan:

ANSI/ASQC Z1.4, normal inspection, level II, single sampling acceptable quality level–1.0 major characteristics and 4.0 for minor characteristics

Quantity accepted: none   Quantity rejected: 500 each

Contract number: N68335-XX-X-XXXX

Description of defect:

Characteristic 1.000" + 0.0000" and –0.001 code number 102 measures 1.001" which is oversize by 0.001".

Cause of the defect:

Examination of the machine that produced the part indicates that the cutting tool is worn. The production lot returned to the manufacturing department for screening and work.

Corrective action taken:

a. Worn cutting tool replaced with a new one.

b. Defective parts reworked to drawing requirement.

c. Production lot resubmitted to the inspection department and all drawing characteristics reinspected and were found to be in compliance with drawing requirements.

d. A recheck of the micrometer that was used to check the part indicates that it was within the instrument's accuracy requirements.

Signature _____ Title _____ Date _____

Figure 5.13 Nonconforming material report.

6

Case Study 2—Supplier's Calibration System

An Integral Part of an ANSI/ISO/ASQ Q9000 Quality System Manual

The selection and application of an appropriate calibration system standard is based on a supplier's own initiative in anticipation of contracts that specify a requirement for the establishment and maintenance of an acceptable calibration system. A system is selected to meet the needs, interests, and expectations of internal and external customers. For this case study, the focus is centered on ISO 10012:2003, *Measurement management systems—Requirements for measurement processes and measuring equipment.*

During the past two decades, several new calibration system standards were introduced to the public by the United States and the world community. All of the following standards—including the Department of Defense MIL-STD-45662A *Calibration System* standard, which is now being overshadowed by the new standards published by ANSI, ISO, and ASQ—provide the supplier with guidance regarding the establishment and maintenance of associated policy and procedures:

- ISO 10012:2003, *Measurement management systems—Requirements for measurement processes and measuring equipment*

- ANSI/NCSL-Z540-1-1994, *Calibration Laboratories and Measuring and Test Equipment—General Requirements*

- ANSI/ISO 17025-1999, *General Requirements for the Competence of Testing and Calibration Laboratories*

- MIL-STD-45662A, *Calibration System Requirements*

It is important to note that since the information in these standards essentially provides the same message, suppliers of metrology services can tailor an existing calibration policy to meet any of these calibration system standards or to address supplementary specification requirements. Examples of such supplementary requirements might include concurrent calibration of measuring instruments between customer and supplier QA representatives or identifying the responsibility and process for the recalibration of customer-supplied M&TE.

Management's Commitment
to Quality Excellence

To meet the needs, interests, and expectations of both internal and external customers, starting with the implementation, maintenance, and continuous improvement of the policies and procedures referenced herein.

John Q. Quality, CEO
XXX Company, Inc.

TABLE OF CONTENTS

RECORD OF CHANGES

Date

Revisions, Additions, and Deletions

5-7-200X

1. Deleted all references to MIL-STD-45662A.

2. Added in its place ISO 10012:2003, *Measurement management systems—Requirements for measurement processes and measuring equipment*

OVERVIEW OF THE CONFIRMATION SYSTEM[1]

The XXX Company is a midsized company staffed with approximately 200 employees that produce mechanical and electromechanical equipment. The company's calibration laboratory, which is the primary source for the calibration of M&TE and secondary standards, is headed by a metrology manager who reports directly to the QA director and has a staff of calibration technicians.

Independent calibration laboratories are solicited to calibrate our MSs and to repair and recalibrate some M&TE. The policies and procedures described herein are issued to control the accuracy of M&TE in accordance with the intent of ISO 10012:2003, *Measurement management systems—Requirements for measurement processes and measuring equipment.*

All inspection, measuring, and test devices used to inspect and test products and services and to assess process improvement techniques are calibrated with higher-level standards of known accuracy. New M&TE is calibrated when the instrument is introduced into the calibration system. These instruments are continually calibrated prior to use until sufficient data is generated to justify an established frequency of recalibration, giving due consideration to the instruments' stability, purpose, discrimination, and degree of usage. The results of each calibration will be entered into the computer system for subsequent statistical analysis, detection of accuracy trends, and adjustment of calibration intervals when appropriate.

Inventory Record of M&TE and MS

An inventory record of all active and inactive measuring instruments, consisting of the following information, is located in a separate calibration procedures manual:

- Instrument nomenclature
- Instrument identification number
- Instrument description and use
- Nominal value
- Accuracy of certified value

- Source of calibration

- Standard procedures

- Instrument manufacturer's written instructions

- Company-prepared instructions

- Calibration procedure number

Inactive or uncalibrated instruments are identified as such. They are stored in an area separate and apart from active gages.

The QA director, with support from auditors, will periodically review the established procedures and processes to verify that they contain complete details for meeting current and future specified requirements of the ISO 10012 standard. Improved procedures based on new external and internal customer requirements and recommendations will be established and implemented as interim changes (see Figure 6.1). Interim changes and other improvements will be included

XXX Company, Inc.
Anytown, USA

Calibration System Procedure

Prepared by* _____ Title _____ Date _____
(Signature)

Reviewed by^^ _____ Title _____ Date _____

Approved by: *** _____ Title _____ Date _____

Distribution:

Copy No.	Recipient
1	Master file
2	QA director
3	Metrology manager
4	Customer

* Metrology manager
** QA director
*** Plant manager

Figure 6.1 Signatures of key quality management personnel.

in the basic quality manual during the annual revision of the complete manual. No changes are valid until they are reviewed by the QA director and approved by the plant manager. When there is a need for new and unfamiliar inspection and test equipment, particularly during product design development, personnel will be provided with necessary training to use the new measuring equipment prior to production of products and services. Only those gages that are properly calibrated shall be made available for use at the respective verification station. Objective quality evidence regarding the accuracy of M&TE and primary and secondary standards shall be made available for review and assessment by the purchaser when so requested.

PLANNING

Calibration systems planning is accomplished by the QA director, the metrology manager, and their staff technicians.[2]

Current Contracts

For add-on contracts associated with products currently produced by the company, the focus shall be centered on whether established policies and processes are up-to-date and readily available when needed.

New Contracts for New Product Designs

For product designs that are new to the company, the metrology manager will be furnished with a list of all drawings, specifications, standards, an abstract of contract quality requirements, and a copy of an established quality plan. The metrology manager shall review these documents to determine the specified product tolerances, M&TE accuracy requirements, and availablity of associate M&TE and MSs from company inventory.

When additional instruments are to be purchased from an outside source, the metrology manager shall include the pertinent calibration system standard requirements and a certified statement regarding the traceability of the supplier's measurement standards to NIST in the requisition to the purchasing manager. The certified statement shall be supported with objective quality evidence. Delivery of calibrated instruments that are in consonance with the company's established milestone schedules shall be included in the purchase order.

PERIODIC AUDIT AND REVIEW OF THE CONFIRMATION SYSTEM

Audits of company procedures, processes, and personnel who implement the calibration system are carried out by a calibration specialist or a team of calibration specialists familiar with the established policies and procedures.[3] Such person, or persons, may be an employee or an accredited third party *not* having specific responsibilities in the department to be audited.

Frequency of Audits

Scheduled audits for all departments that support calibration systems management are conducted at least once a year. Unscheduled audits that are performed more frequently than once a year are motivated by contract change notices, continuous process improvement recommendations, and customer complaints.

Reports

Reports regarding audit observations are documented and reported to the QA director with appropriate recommendations for process improvements. The QA director will assure that audit recommendations for improvements are implemented and properly maintained.

MEASURING EQUIPMENT[4]

MSs

Standards used by an independent calibration laboratory to calibrate the company's MSs shall have the accuracy, stability, range, and resolution to ensure that required measurement areas of acceptance are maintained.

Traceability

Independent laboratory standards that are used to calibrate the measuring equipment shall have a higher level of accuracy of at least 10 times greater than the company's working standards. Primary and secondary standards are traceable by an unbroken chain of calibration events to NIST or an international standard.

The accuracy of the company's standards is 10 times greater than the accuracy of the company's M&TE and is traceable to NIST. Accuracy ratio between the M&TE that is used to inspect and test products is 4:1 or greater than the product's tightest tolerance. (Note: Specific accuracy ratios are contained in each instrument's calibration procedure.)

UNCERTAINTY OF MEASUREMENTS[5]

(Accuracy ratios of area of acceptance and area of uncertainty)

Laboratory Standards

All of the company's standards are calibrated by an independent calibration laboratory with known capabilities. The metrology manager will assure that the purchase orders will include, in the statement of work, that company standards will be calibrated with higher-level standards that have an accuracy ratio of at least 10 times better than the instrument being calibrated with an area of uncertainty no greater than 10 percent. The statement of work also includes a requirement for the independent calibration laboratory to furnish a certified calibration report showing a list of actual measurements and the actual area (value) of uncertainty. The metrology manager or his or her designated representative reviews the laboratory's certificate and documents evidence of acceptance (or nonacceptance) by applying his or her signature or inspection stamp to the certificate.

Company Standards

The accuracy ratio between the company's MSs and its M&TE shall be 10:1. Company standards that are found to have an area of uncertainty greater than 10 percent are replaced with a standard that is in compliance with the pertinent calibration procedure. The replaced standard will be repaired, recalibrated, or downgraded.

M&TE and Product Tolerance

The area of uncertainty of working M&TE in relation to an associated product characteristic tolerance is in accordance with the appropriate quality plan. The area of uncertainty shall be between 10 and 25 percent. Technicians and inspectors refer to the applicable product and calibration procedure when determining the appropriate accuracy ratio between instrument accuracy and the product tolerance. When calibration data show a negative trend in an area of uncertainty, the metrology manager or his or her designated representative shall investigate the cause of this trend and take appropriate action.

CUMULATIVE EFFECT OF UNCERTAINTIES[6]

All calibration procedures shall address the cumulative effect that the instrument's area of uncertainty has on products and services produced for customers. The cumulative effect of the uncertainties regarding each stage of the chain of calibrations—from primary and secondary standards to working the M&TE to the product tolerance—shall be maintained as follows:

- The accuracy ratio between laboratory standards and the company's secondary standards shall be 10:1 or greater.

- The accuracy ratio between the company standards and working measuring and test equipment shall be 10:1 or greater.

- The accuracy ratio between the company's inspection equipment and M&TE and the product tolerance shall be from 4:1 to 10:1. (Selected accuracy ratios or modifications thereto are contained in the respective quality plan.)

When an area of uncertainty is found to be greater than the value specified in the respective calibration procedure (or one that has is found to have an area of acceptance less than the value specified in the calibration procedure), the instrument shall be removed from the calibration area and recalibrated, followed by an investigation as to its impact on the products and services that were previously released to the next operation, to storage, to the shipping department, or to the customer or user. For example, a working instrument with an accuracy ratio of 4:1 whose area of uncertainty is found to be greater than 25 percent will require an investigation to determine the adequacy of established calibration procedures as well as the quality status of products and services previously accepted. Similarly, a standard instrument with an accuracy ratio 10:1 whose area of uncertainty is found to be greater that 10 percent will require an investigation to determine the adequacy of established calibration procedures as well as verifying the accuracy of M&TE previously calibrated.

DOCUMENTED CONFIRMATION PROCEDURES[7]

There are three sources of calibration procedures that are used by the company:

1. Standard calibration procedures that are available from GIDEP

2. Instrument manufacturer's recommended calibration procedures

3. Company-prepared procedures

Calibration procedures prepared by the company shall include the following:

- Original or revision date

- Instrument nomenclature

- Calibration procedure number

- Accuracy of instrument to be calibrated

- Instrument range

- Instrument discrimination

- Measurement standard(s)
- Step-by-step procedure
- Name of originator, title of originator, and date

RECORDS[8]

Records are contained on the following documents:

1. An abstract of contract quality requirements, which includes:

   - Contract or purchase order number
   - Contract or purchase order change notices
   - Description of supplies and services solicited or offered
   - First-article inspection, when appropriate, and delivery date
   - Concurrent inspection and acceptance with the customer's QA representative when appropriate
   - Item number
   - Quantity
   - Delivery dates
   - Copy of, or source of, drawings, specifications, standards, and other contract quality requirements, such as tailoring and supplementary requirements
   - Name of the originator of the abstract, title of the abstract, and date

2. Calibration equipment list, which includes:

   - Name of the instrument
   - Nominal size
   - Accuracy value
   - Quantity

- Application (primary standard, secondary standard, or working M&TE)

3. Master requirements list, which includes:
   - Product nomenclature and part number
   - Product characteristic code number
   - Measuring device used to inspect and test the product
   - Measuring device identification number
   - Measuring device code number

4. Instrument calibration record, which includes:
   - Instrument nomenclature
   - Model number
   - Identification number
   - Accuracy of the instrument
   - Procedure number
   - Resolution value
   - Calibration frequency
   - Characteristic identification
   - Work performance
   - Characteristic identification
   - Measured value

5. Observation record, which includes but is not limited to:
   - Product characteristics and/or code number
   - Measuring device that was used to check the product characteristic
   - Measuring device code number

6. Recall/location record, which includes:
   - Instrument nomenclature
   - Identification number

- Calibration frequency
- Item location
- Date recalled
- Calibration date
- Assigned to
- Date in service
- Assigned by
- Remarks as appropriate

7. Calibration status labels, which include:

- Last calibration date
- Calibration due date
- By whom calibrated

8. Nonconforming M&TE tag, which identifies:

- Date
- Department
- Instrument nomenclature
- Instrument identification number
- Quantity
- Instruments that are out of tolerance
- Brief description of out-of-tolerance condition
- Associated contract or purchase order number
- Signature and date of the person who originated the complaint

9. Metrology deficiency report, which includes:

- Instrument nomenclature
- Originator of the report
- Recipient of the report

- Report number and date
- Description of the measuring device
- Calibration procedure number
- Reply due date
- Signature of the originator
- Description of the out-of-tolerance condition
- Reply as to cause
- Recommended action
- Investigator's signature, investigator's title, and the date

10. MRB report, which includes:

- Instrument identification number
- Product name and identification number
- Specification number
- Drawing number
- Calibration procedure number
- Number of instruments reported out of tolerance
- Department and verification station
- Vendor (when appropriate)
- Description of complaint
- Frequency of the complaint
- Originator of the complaint
- Date complaint submitted to MRB
- Name and title of MRB members
- Assignment of recommended corrective action
- Action required
- Follow-up date
- Signatures and titles of MRB members

- Recipients of copies of MRB findings (key management personnel)

11. Corrective-action record, which includes:

    - Originator of the request for corrective action
    - Recipient of the information
    - Instrument nomenclature and identification number
    - Number of instruments received
    - Number of defective instruments
    - Disposition

12. Vendor performance history, which includes:

    - ANSI/ISO/ASQ Q9000 registration and certification
    - Distribution to personnel who have a need to know
    - Name and address of the vendor being tracked
    - Date capabilities originally verified
    - Record of past performance
    - Date
    - Contract or purchase order number
    - Instrument identification number
    - Quantity rejected
    - Comment (enter as appropriate)
    - Vendor qualification
    - Corrective action required
    - Seek other sources

13. Employee training record (metrology), which includes:

    - Employee's name, employee's address, and the date
    - Calibration capabilities
    - Calibration systems management capabilities
    - Required company training

- List of skills and years of experience
- Future training plans
- Person responsible for monitoring the training

NONCONFORMING MEASURING EQUIPMENT[9]

A record of M&TE that is out of tolerance will be clearly identified on a nonconforming M&TE tag. The information contained on this tag shall include the date, quantity, department, instrument identification number, brief description of nonconformity, associated contract or purchase order number, and the signature and title of the person who reported the complaint.

Company M&TE

All nonconforming instruments will be placed in a designated holding area specifically selected for discrepant instruments. No one is authorized to remove nonconforming instruments from the holding area until satisfactory corrective action is taken by the metrology manager. The MRB shall support the corrective-action process and the disposition of nonconforming instruments when the complaint involves products and services previously accepted with instruments of questionable accuracy.

Significant out-of-tolerance conditions, which adversely affect product and service quality, shall be documented on a metrology deficiency report and corrected within 10 working days. Follow-up action shall be taken by the metrology manager to verify satisfactory implementation of recommended corrective action. This action shall be taken within seven days after resolution of the deficiency.

Inspection and Test Equipment Furnished to Subcontractors

When complaints are received from subcontractors regarding the receipt of out-of-tolerance M&TE furnished by the company, an immediate investigation will be undertaken by the customer complaint department representative to determine whether the complaint is justified. When a complaint is found to be justified, the following actions shall be taken:

- Examine company calibration records for any indication of nonconformity and, at the same time, request that the instrument be returned to the company for assessment and necessary action. If this is impractical, arrangements shall be made for an investigation of the complaint by a representative of the metrology department at the subcontractor's facility.

- Recalibrate the instrument to determine the actual out-of-tolerance conditions.

- Submit a report of findings to the QA director.

- Recalibrate the instrument or replace it with one of known accuracy.

- Determine the adequacy of established calibration procedures.

- Determine whether calibration intervals should be shortened.

- Determine whether the instrument should be calibrated prior to use.

If the reported complaint was detected after product and service assessments, determine the impact that the out-of-tolerance condition has on products and services accepted with the instruments in question. Follow-up action shall be taken by the QA department on corrective action taken on internal and external complaints to verify that satisfactory corrective action was taken.

CONFIRMATION LABELING[10]

The confirmation status of the M&TE used to inspect and test products and services is identified on labels or tags. Where practical, the following information shall be referenced on each label or tag:

- Date of calibration

- Due date for next calibration

- Person responsible for calibration

- For limited-use instruments, the instrument's acceptable range

- Person responsible for confirmation

- Compensating correction factors, when appropriate

When it is impractical to label an instrument, the confirmation status shall be identified on its container. Color coding is used instead of labels or tags when the small size or functional characteristics of the instrument precludes container marking, labels, or tags. Color coding provides only the year and month that the instrument is due for recalibration. The exact due date for the calibration is contained in the instrument's calibration procedures. An example of a color-coding scheme is:

Year	Color Code (First Dot)
20XX	Violet
20XX	Blue
20XX	Green
20XX	Gray
20XX	Orange
20XX	Yellow
20XX	Red
20XX	Brown
20XX	Black

Month	Color Code (Second Dot)
January	Black
February	Brown
March	Red
April	Yellow
May	Orange
June	Gray
July	Green
August	Blue
September	Violet
October	White
November	Gold
December	Silver

Computer-generated data that lists the instruments' nomenclature, identification numbers, and calibration due dates are furnished to technicians on the first working day of the month for review and identification of exact calibration due dates. Obsolete and out-of-service instruments will be placed in a locked storage cabinet or storage area and identified as such to ensure that uncalibrated measuring equipment will not be used until properly calibrated. Personally owned M&TE, which includes employee, independent-consultant, and independent-laboratory instruments, will be used only when approved by the QC manager.

When the use of personally owned equipment is authorized, the equipment will be labeled in accordance with established company policy and maintained in accordance with procedures referenced herein. Externally calibrated M&TE will be identified in accordance with the statement of work provisions referenced in the contract or purchase order.

SEALING FOR INTEGRITY[11]

Tamper-resistant seals shall be affixed to operator-accessible adjustments that, if moved, will affect the calibration of the M&TE or MS. The QA director, with support from the customer's QA representative when appropriate, shall identify instruments that require seals based on their experience regarding how the instruments are used in support of contract quality requirements. The calibration technician or agency shall verify that instruments are removed from use if the seals are found broken.

INTERVALS OF CONFIRMATION[12]

Intervals of confirmation of M&TE and MSs are assigned and maintained by the metrology manager and his or her staff of calibration technicians. The intervals are based on stability, purpose, and degree of usage. A list of MSs and working instruments is located in the company's procedures manual. Instruments are always calibrated with higher-level standards of known accuracy. Each unit of M&TE is calibrated prior to use when:

- First introduced to the calibration system

- The unit is inactive over an extended period of time

- There is evidence of damage or mishandling

The introduction of a calibration interval is predicated on objective quality evidence generated during previous calibrations. Intervals of confirmation shall be shortened only when the record reflects a favorable calibration history. A recall system is maintained by the metrology department to ensure that active instruments will be calibrated prior to use or in accordance with an established calibration frequency. The recall record is maintained in the respective recall/location record form.

Regarding instruments that are on an established interval of confirmation, department supervisors will be notified of instruments that are overdue for recalibration via internal communication procedures (e-mail, memo, and so on). A temporary extension of calibration due dates may be authorized only when a favorable in-tolerance history of calibrations is in evidence and the product associated with the pertinent instrument will not be shipped to the customer until the instrument in question is recalibrated and been found to be in tolerance and properly recorded.

USE OF OUTSIDE PRODUCTS AND SERVICES[13]

The QA director and the metrology manager will support the purchasing manager when soliciting capable outside calibration sources. All purchase requisitions are reviewed by the metrology manager for adequacy and approved by the QA director. The purchasing department will assure that all delegated calibration system requirements are made known to the subcontractor or vendor. The purchase order will reflect a clear description of supplies and services including (as appropriate):

- Specifications

- Drawings

- Calibration system requirements

- Requirement for qualification

- Calibration instructions

- Feedback data (reports and certifications)

An employee from the QC department conducts an on-site assessment of the proposed supplier's QA capabilities before a purchase order is issued for solicited instruments and/or calibration services under the following conditions:

- The supplier did not achieve ANSI/ISO/ASQ Q9000 certification and registration status.

- In the company's files, there is no history that indicates subcontractor/vendor capabilities.

- A supplier does not have an established reputation within the industry to indicate acceptable capabilities.

STORAGE AND HANDLING[14]

Company-Owned M&TE and MS

All instruments shall be stored, handled, and transported in such a manner as to protect them from damage, deterioration, and wear. Active as well as out-of-service instruments will be stored in separate containers to protect them from physical damage. Each measuring surface shall be cleaned with a lint-free cloth prior to use. In areas requiring protection against rust, surfaces shall be coated with a film of corrosion-resistant oil when those areas are not in use. When necessary, the instruments will be wrapped in moisture-free barrier material before they are placed in storage. Both company-supplied and customer-supplied M&TE shall be visually examined by the calibration technician and inspectors prior to use to detect out-of-tolerance conditions caused by improper handling or storage.

CUSTOMER-SUPPLIED M&TE AND MS

Customer-supplied instruments shall be examined upon receipt for corrosion and physical damage. Instruments found to be unserviceable for use will be recorded and reported to the customer. Instruments received in good condition will be handled and stored the same as company-owned instruments.

TRACEABILITY[15]

One of the fundamental requirements of the calibration system is the ability to ensure traceability of the M&TE and MSs via an unbroken chain of calibrations to NIST or an international standard. However, since the company does not do business directly with NIST or any international laboratory, the company's focus will be centered on the independent laboratory that calibrates the company's standards. It is from these standards that the metrology department calibrates all working instruments. The director of purchasing, with support from the QA director, shall ensure that purchase orders that are issued to an independent laboratory contain the following feedback data:

- Required calibration system standard
- Item nomenclature
- Identification of the appropriate calibration system standards
- Certificate number
- NIST report number
- Date of calibration
- Identification of nominal characteristics checked
- Identification of measured values
- Areas of uncertainty
- Relevant conditions (environment under which stated values were obtained)

- Statement that calibrations were conducted with measurement standards traceable to a national or international standard

- Signature and title of an authorized representative of the calibration laboratory and the date

The metrology manager or a designated representative shall validate certificates and reports associated with a calibrated instrument by applying his or her signature to the certificate or report before it is filed. Files are held at least three years or as many years as specified by the customer. Files are routed to the director of purchasing via the QA director for necessary action when the certificate or report is found to be nonconforming. Certificates or reports of calibration shall be kept readily accessible to internal and external customers. As part of an investigation regarding the traceability of a nonconforming product or service, both the customer-complaint monitor and the owner of the associated process check the quality plan to make sure that specified technical requirements were properly addressed.

ENVIRONMENTAL CONTROLS[16]

Obtaining the accuracy of inspection, measuring, and test instruments within a controlled environment will be accomplished to the extent necessary to maintain detrimental conditions within acceptable limits of the calibration being performed. When appropriate, adequate compensating corrections shall be made. In addition, the following conditions shall be maintained:

- Calibration stations shall be free from extraneous equipment and supplies.

- Storage and holding areas shall be kept in an orderly manner.

- Technicians must wipe measuring surfaces with a lint-free cloth or commercial paper wipe before each measurement.

- Benches and other calibration surfaces shall be sufficiently free from vibration so that readings can be consistently obtained to an accuracy of at least the value indicated for each reading.

- Relative humidity conditions shall range between 35 and 55 percent.

- Temperature conditions shall be maintained from 67.5°F to 68.5°F for reference standards and from 68°F to 73°F for working standards.

- Lighting shall be 80 foot-candles at bench tops.

PERSONNEL[17]

Management

The functions of calibration systems management are assigned to personnel who have achieved certification status from an accredited third party (see Figure 6.2).

Technicians

Calibration technicians will qualify to work within the metrology department after they have completed six-month internal training, after they have at least five years' experience in precision measurement with a previous employer, or if they are certified by an accredited agency (see Figure 6.2).

Documentation of metrology policy and procedures is an imperative for promoting a clear understanding of calibration systems requirements. This documentation helps to ensure that they are appropriately coordinated with personnel associated with quality systems in design, development, production, installation, and servicing.

Employee Training Record

(Metrology)

Name _____ Date _____

Home address _____

1. *Calibration capabilities*

Discipline	Qualified Yes No	If yes, source of training Certified Formal Previous employer
Mechanical	— —	— — —
Electrical	— —	— — —
Electronic	— —	— — —
Pneumatic	— —	— — —
Hydraulic	— —	— — —
Force	— —	— — —
Certified mechanical inspector		Yes __ No __
Certified quality technician		Yes __ No __

2. *Calibration systems management capabilities*

Certified quality engineer	Yes	No __
Certified reliability and maintainability engineer	Yes __	No __
Professional engineer in the discipline of quality	Yes __	No __

3. *Required company training*

		If no, scheduled training date
Policy procedures	Yes __ No __	_____
Calibration procedures	Yes __ No __	_____
Written processes	Yes __ No __	_____
Work instructions	Yes __ No __	_____
Intern program	Yes __ No __	_____

4. List of skills and years of experience

_____

5. Future training plans

_____

Training monitor

Figure 6.2 Record of employee training.

ENDNOTES

1. ISO 10012:2003, *Measurement management systems—Requirements for measurement processes and measuring equipment,* clause 5.1.
2. Ibid., clause 5.4.
3. Ibid., clause 8.2.1.
4. Ibid., clause 6.3.1.
5. Ibid., clause 7.1.1.
6. Ibid., clause 7.1.1.
7. Ibid., clause 6.2.1.
8. Ibid., clause 7.1.4.
9. Ibid., clause 8.3.2.
10. Ibid., clause 6.2.4.
11. Ibid., clause 7.1.3.
12. Ibid., clause 7.1.2.
13. Ibid., clause 6.4.
14. Ibid., clause 6.3.1.
15. Ibid., clause 7.3.2.
16. Ibid., clause 6.3.2.
17. Ibid., clause 6.1.1.

7

Costs Associated with Metrology Systems Management

> *Total quality costs is intended to represent the difference between the actual cost of a product or service and what the costs would be if the quality was perfect. It is, as previously ascribed to Juran, "gold in the mine," just waiting to be extracted. When you zero in on the elimination of failure costs and then challenge the level of appraisal costs, you will not only be managing the cost of quality, you will be mining gold.*[1]

The control of quality costs is another option available to a product manufacturer or independent calibration laboratory for measuring the effectiveness of a metrology system. Two points of leverage can be attacked by metrology professionals in conjunction with management. These points can be found in the proper assessment of contract requirements and the monitoring of actions associated with 10 critical quality elements through the proper application of the procedures specified in the preceding chapters. Basic to cost control, credibility, and customer service is the control of out-of-tolerance conditions, which involves the actions of the metrology professional.

EFFECTIVE USE OF THE CONTRACT OR TECHNICAL SPECIFICATIONS

When contract requirements are clearly defined and distributed in a timely fashion, the planning process between the procurement office's contract administrator and the prime contractor is enhanced and the operation becomes cost-effective. As described in chapter 1, the contract and its associated drawings and documentation are fertile areas for the introduction of costly and compromising errors of omission. Clarity and a careful system for communicating specifications and work changes can dramatically affect profitability and the delivery of a quality product.

There are two ways that the metrology professional can possibly use the contract or technical specifications to avoid unnecessary work and avoid rework. These are the proper understanding of complex and critical items and the proper application of intervals of calibration. (Complex and critical items and calibration intervals might or might not be specified in the contract or technical specifications.) It is important for the metrology professional to have a clear idea regarding which standards are to be applied and to have a clear rationale for their application. The decision to apply complex or critical items and the decision regarding intervals of calibration influence the cost as well as the validity of the calibration system.

Complex and Critical Items

Complex items have quality characteristics, not wholly visible in the end item, for which contractual conformance must be established progressively through precise measurements, tests, and controls applied during purchasing, manufacturing, performance, assembly, and functional operation either as an individual item or in conjunction with other items. Noncomplex items have quality characteristics for which simple measurements and test of the end item are sufficient to determine conformance to contractual requirements.[2]

A critical application of an item is one in which failure of the item could injure people or jeopardize a vital mission. A critical item can be either *peculiar,* meaning it has only one application, or *common,* meaning it has multiple applications. A noncritical application is any other application. Noncritical items may also be peculiar or common.[3]

Products associated with a complex product design require an extensive and diversified amount of measuring instruments. Therefore, these products present many opportunities to improve the processes and procedures associated with metrology systems management.

A critical application of a product is normally associated with items that are classified as complex. Aircraft flight recorders and naval radar systems are two examples of complex, critical items. Each item requires sophisticated measuring equipment to check the component parts, check the subassemblies, and perform functional testing of the end item. These items are critical to their assigned missions as well as to protecting the safety and lives of the personnel who use them.

Intervals of Calibration

One the most promising areas for cost savings in the metrology system lies in the establishment, application, and maintenance of objective calibration intervals. There are no restrictions placed on metrology managers as to what methodology to use to establish an interval of calibration that satisfactorily meets a reliability target or how to adjust a calibration interval if the desired reliability is not being met. Specific intervals of calibration for inspection equipment, M&TE, and MSs can be established contractually by a calibration laboratory that is located in the manufacturer's facility or by an independent calibration laboratory. Whatever the source, the supplier of the metrology service must demonstrate that each instrument is calibrated and traceable to objective quality evidence.

IMPACT OF OUT-OF-TOLERANCE CONDITIONS

Significant out-of-tolerance conditions (see chapter 2) add costs to the bottom line that were not anticipated during the preparation of an original quality plan. The costs can include the following:

• Costs can be incurred from investigating the out-of-tolerance condition and from implementing the appropriate corrective action at all internal and external calibration stations where the instruments in question were calibrated or used.

• The man-hours needed to verify the accuracy of the M&TE and to reinspect products that were inspected during in-process and final-inspection operations can add cost to the project.

• When a contract stipulates that final inspection and acceptance shall be at the destination, the costs incurred for this function are absorbed by the prime contractor. However, when the product is found to be defective, the costs to screen, cull, repair, reject, and/or replace the product are usually absorbed by the product manufacturer.

• Costs can be incurred from processing a request for waiver regarding a product deficiency that does not adversely impact form, fit, or function.

• Expenses can be incurred from determining whether or not the products shipped to the customer comply with contractual requirements.

• Costs can be realized from reviewing the calibration procedures and from upgrading existing or preparing new calibration procedures.

IMPACT OF IN-TOLERANCE CONDITIONS

In-tolerance conditions that are supported with objective quality evidence provide quality systems managers with information that can justify a decision to lengthen a calibration interval and therefore reduce costs to calibrate instruments. Sharing the cost savings with the customer in subsequent procurements can lead to significant costs savings over an extended period of time for both parties. In-tolerance conditions can also reduce the supplier's risk of producing nonconforming products and reduce the purchaser's risk of receiving nonconforming products.

Suppliers of products and services are cautioned not to calibrate inspection equipment and M&TE at an established interval for an extended period of time without taking advantage of the opportunity that is presented to them when documented calibration data allows them to lengthen an interval of calibration and at the same time save time and money without compromising instrument accuracy. Some suppliers live with an attitude of, "Why should I change calibration intervals when I know that my instruments are accurate and reliable every time we calibrate them?"

This perception is not in consonance with a cost-effective operation because every time a calibration interval is justifiably lengthened, there is a reduction of man-hours as well a reduction of costs to calibrate inspection, measuring, and test instruments. Conversely, when calibration records conclusively indicate a significant out-of-tolerance condition, intervals of calibration will normally have to be shortened and costs to calibrate will escalate. Figures 7.1 through 7.4 show how calibration costs are reduced when an interval of calibration is justifiably lengthened and how unanticipated calibration costs are added to the bottom line when an interval of calibration is shortened.* Figures 7.1 through 7.4 use the following factors:

- Duration of calibration of one instrument (DCOI)
- Hourly rate of the technician (HRT)
- Calibration interval (CI)
- Number of like instuments (NLI)

---

* Figures 7.1 through 7.4 are intended to show comparison costs when a calibration interval is changed. These examples don't imply that all these changes can be made in the same calender year; rather, they show the effects that interval changes have on calibration costs when intervals are lengthened or shortened over a certain period of time. These examples pertain to one instrument; however, cost savings can be further appreciated when an interval of calibration is justifiably lengthened for two or more similar instruments with the same accuracy requirements and the same calibration interval.

Formula: NLI × DCOI × HRT × CI = Yearly costs to calibrate M&TE

Factors:

CI = Various (see table below)
NLI = 1
DCOI = 2 hours
HRT = $20.00

$$\text{NLI} \times \text{DCOI} \times \text{HRT} \times \text{CI}$$
$$= 1 \times 2 \times 20 \times 12$$
$$= \$480$$

DCOI = 2 hours
HRT = $20.00

Comparison of yearly costs to calibrate one instrument when intervals are lengthened

Number of Like items	Calibration Interval*	Number of Yearly Calibrations	Required Man-Hours	Yearly Cost to Calibrate
1	1	12.0	24.0	$480
1	2	6.0	12.0	240
1	3	4.0	8.0	160
1	4	3.0	6.0	120
1	5	2.4	4.8	96
1	6	2.0	4.0	80
1	7	1.7	3.4	68
1	8	1.5	3.0	60
1	9	1.3	2.6	52
1	10	1.2	2.4	48
1	11	1.09	2.18	44
1	12	1.0	1.0	20

*Monthly

Figure 7.1 Impact of lengthened calibration intervals.

EFFECTIVE USE OF
CALIBRATION INTERVALS

Savvy metrology managers recognize that the establishment of calibration intervals is an area in which costs to calibrate inspection, measuring, and test instruments can escalate. This escalation generally occcurs when proper consideration is not given to the degree of usage, instrument accuracy, type of standard or equipment, required precision, and other conditions that adversely affect the measurement process, such as the environment in which an instrument is processed. Effective managers also recognize that

Comparison of monthly costs to calibrate one instrument when intervals are lengthened

Interval Frequency	— Months												Number of Yearly Intervals
	1	2	3	4	5	6	7	8	9	10	11	12	
1-	100	x	x	x	x	x	x	x	x	x	x	x	12.0
2-		50	-	x	-	x	-	x	-	x	-	x	6.0
3-			33.3	-	-	x	-	-	x	-	-	x	4.0
4-				25	-	-	-	x	-	-	-	x	3.0
5-					20	-	-	-	-	x	-	-	2.4
6-						16.7	-	-	-	-	-	x	2.0
7-							14.2	-	-	-	-	-	1.7
8-								12.5	-	-	-	-	1.5
9-									11	-	-	x	1.3
10-										10.8	-	-	1.2
11-											9.2	-	1.1
12-												8.3	1.0

Percent

Figure 7.2 Percent of yearly costs when intervals are *lengthened*.

DOCI = 2 Hours
HRT = $20.00
(One item)

Comparison of yearly costs to calibrate one instrument when intervals are shortened

Interval Frequency*	Number of Yearly Calibrations	Required Man-Hours	Yearly Cost to Calibrate
12	1.0	1.0	$20
11	1.09	2.18	44
10	2.1	2.4	48
9	1.2	2.6	52
8	1.5	3.0	60
7	1.7	3.4	58
6	2.0	4.0	80
5	2.4	4.8	96
4	3.0	6.0	120
3	4.0	8.0	160
2	6.0	12.0	240
1	12.0	24.0	480

*Monthly

Figure 7.3 Impact of shortened calibration *intervals*.

Comparison of monthly costs to calibrate one instrument when intervals are shortened

Interval Frequency	Months												Number of Yearly Intervals
	1	2	3	4	5	6	7	8	9	10	11	12	
12–												8.3	1.0
11–											9.2	–	1.1
10–										10	–	–	1.2
9–									10.8	–	–	–	1.3
8–								12.5	–	–	–	–	1.5
7–							14.2	–	–	–	–	–	1.7
6–						16.7	–	–	–	–	–	x	2.0
5–					20	–	–	–	–	x	–	x	2.4
4–				25	–	–	–	x	–	–	–	x	3.0
3–			33.3	–	–	x	–	–	x	–	–	x	4.0
2–		50	–	x	–	x	–	x	–	x	–	x	6.0
1–	100	x	x	x	x	x	x	x	x	x	x	x	12.0

Percent

Figure 7.4   Percent of yearly costs when intervals are *shortened*.

when data associated with an established calibration interval is periodically reviewed and intervals are adjusted accordingly (lengthened or shortened), reliability targets will be met and a positive impact on quality costs will be present.

These managers continuously monitor items that reduce cost escalation while contributing to the delivery of a quality product (see chapter 3). The managers also make sure that:

• Calibration intervals are adequate to provide required confidence regarding instrument accuracy.

• Inspection department personnel are prohibited from using inspection, measuring, and test instruments that are past their calibration due dates without referring the matter for preliminary assessment or to an MRB for adjudication (see chapter 5).

• Inspection departments are prohibited from using inspection, measuring, and test instruments that are past their due dates for calibration without permission granted to the supplier from its customer. Such cases carry the proviso that the instruments in question are to be recalibrated for accuracy before the applicable production lot is shipped from the supplier's shipping department or sent to its next destination within the company.

Good judgment is an important part of any process. Experience has shown that suppliers can, at times, add unnecessary costs to the bottom line through overkill. Even though data analysis and recalibrations indicate stability and accuracy of inspection equipment and M&TE, the supplier elects *not* to shorten a calibration interval when such action might be quite appropriate. For example, a supplier might elect to:

- Calibrate daily when weekly is acceptable

- Calibrate weekly when monthly is acceptable

- Calibrate instruments on an established calibration interval when the prior-to-use method is more appropriate

The intelligent, documented, and applied methods for decisions regarding intervals of calibration produce the desired objective for the metrology professional. That objective is controlling unnecessary costs while producing a product that is free of defects.

TEN-ELEMENT CHECKLIST

Ten critical elements of a metrology system and related factors that have a direct impact on the costs associated with the establishment, implementation, and maintenance of a calibration system are listed on the following pages. This checklist is designed to be a practical, working tool to bring the metrology system together by joining efficiency with effectiveness. The checklist should be used by management and operations to self-evaluate the organization and its relevant vendors to hold the system accountable. Try using the checklist to examine current capabilities and needs. It should serve as a catalyst for improvement goals and for the recognition and ongoing monitoring of achievement.

1. *Personnel.* The factors include:

   - Metrology management personnel are consistently familiar with detailed contractual requirements and associated drawings, specifications, and standards.

   - Personnel performing calibration systems management have defined responsibility, authority, and organizational freedom to identify and evaluate metrology problems.

   - Employees are encouraged to provide suggestions and recommendations that will improve established calibration policy, procedures, and associated processes.

- Employees receive ongoing training regarding the application of complex procedures and work instructions.

- The supplier ensures that there is clear communication of contract and technical requirements at all levels of metrology management.

- The supplier ensures that qualified personnel are on hand to administer the metrology program.

- The supplier identifies training needs of its metrology management personnel and provides timely training to its personnel where required.

2. *Quality plan.* The factors include:

   - A written quality plan exists.

   - The plan is capable of addressing all of the technical requirements specified in a contractual agreement between two parties, or a system for handling exceptions is in place.

   - The plan addresses requirements for special inspection and test equipment, tooling, and skills.

   - The quality plan addresses tailored specification requirements that have a direct bearing on the selection of special inspection and test equipment.

   - The plan provides procedures for comparing new contract or purchase order requirements with previously prepared metrology procedures and processes and for making changes where appropriate.

   - The plan addresses the need for acquiring new facilities and inspection and measuring equipment when required.

   - Work instructions referenced in the plan are consistently defined and are all-inclusive.

   - The plan describes the method for recording calibration measurements (variable and/or attributes data).

   - The plan defines the acceptable environmental conditions under which calibration measurements are taken and identifies the method for identifying these conditions.

   - The supplier ensures that the customer's prescribed calibration system is compatible with products and services offered.

- The supplier's established procedures provide for the adequacy, currentness, and completeness of tailored specifications, processes, or work instructions related to the metrology program.

3. *Control of documentation.* The factors include:

   - Procedures for documenting the adequacy, completeness, and currentness of the drawings, specifications, and standards that are in place.

   - The control of design changes that impact the metrology system is documented.

   - The effective dates of contract notices associated with metrology requirements are identified.

   - Superseded documents that impact the performance of inspection equipment and M&TE are removed from the production area.

   - Changes to drawings and/or specifications and associated documentation that impact the metrology system are furnished to the prime contractor's designated subcontractors.

   - Documented metrology data is reviewed by management for reliability and improvement on a regularly scheduled basis.

   - Documented calibration inspection records are reviewed and analyzed to identify problem areas.

   - Responsibility and schedule for review are explicit.

   - The supplier documents an individual record for each measuring instrument and MS that addresses:

      - A description and identification of measuring equipment

      - Calibration interval

      - Calibrated due date

      - Identification of calibration source

      - Calibration procedure

      - Calibration results

- Out-of-tolerance conditions

- Compensating correction of measurements (where appropriate)

4. *Control of inspection, measuring, and test instruments.* The factors include:

- The supplier recognizes that a 4:1 or higher accuracy level between inspection and measuring equipment and the product characteristic is imperative for checking product quality.

- The supplier recognizes that a 10:1 accuracy level or higher between MSs and working M&TE is an important element of a calibration procedure.

- Accuracy ratios between MSs and working gages are always kept within acceptable areas.

- Significant out-of-tolerance condition levels are identified.

- Calibration intervals are predicated on the degree of usage or as designated in a contractual agreement between purchaser and supplier.

- Calibration procedures are revised when appropriate, and new calibration procedures are prepared when needed.

- Capability of new providers of metrology services is verified before a purchase order is issued.

- A procedure for the handling and storage of measuring instruments is established and followed consistently to ensure that accuracies are maintained.

- M&TE that is used to verify that supplies conform to contract quality requirements is adequately maintained and controlled in accordance with specified requirements.

- The accuracy of M&TE is verified against a certified MS.

- The prime contractor verifies subcontractor calibration system capabilities.

- The calibration system is coordinated with other QA systems where it impacts the accuracy of M&TE and MSs.

- M&TE is properly handled, stored, transported, and protected from corrosion.

- M&TE and MSs are labeled to indicate calibration status.

- Measuring instruments are calibrated to their full capability.

- Measuring instruments having limitations of use are labeled or limitations are identified.

- Instructions for the use of tamper-resistant seals and disposition of items whose seals are broken are provided.

5. *Nonconforming products and services.* The factors include:

- An effective system for controlling nonconforming material, which includes procedures for identification, segregation, and disposition of nonconforming products and metrology services, is in place.

- Procedures provide for the positive identification of nonconforming M&TE.

- Nonconforming products are reworked and measuring instruments are repaired using documented procedures that are acceptable to both internal and external customers.

- Nonconforming M&TE are processed via preliminary review and, when necessary, via an MRB.

- A report of the costs associated with scrap and rework of products attributed to out-of-tolerance M&TE is maintained by the supplier and provided to the metrology manager.

6. *Corrective action.* The factors include:

- A documented corrective-action procedure is in place.

- Causes of deficiencies attributed to out-of-tolerance M&TE are eliminated.

- The prime contractor ensures that the subcontractors recalibrate M&TE that is found to be out of tolerance.

- Procedures associated with nonconforming products and services include a requirement for the investigation of the metrology procedures, the measuring equipment that was used to inspect the product, and the related calibration data to determine:

   – The impact on products previously produced

   – The need for employee training

   – The prevention of subsequent nonconforming products or services

   – The need to improve established procedures and work instructions

   – The identification of required corrective action

   – The effectiveness of corrective action taken

7. *Control of purchases.* The factors include:

- Verification of product quality via the assessment of data furnished by suppliers.

- Effectiveness, integrity, and control of measuring instruments used by subcontractors are monitored at intervals consistent with the complexity of the end item.

- Metrology test reports, certificates, and other suitable evidence furnished by an independent calibration laboratory are monitored and evaluated to ensure that services are provided in accordance with purchase agreements.

8. *Customer-supplied products.* The factors include:

- The product and measuring instrument are examined upon receipt to detect any functional damage related to poor transportation or handling.

- Periodic inspection of stored M&TE is conducted to ensure adequate protection from damage.

- Measuring surfaces are preserved and protected from corrosion.

- The organization (customer or supplier) that is responsible for recalibration and maintenance of instrument accuracy is clearly identified.

9. *Inspection and testing.* The factors include:

- Inspection and testing records that are traceable to M&TE are used to check product characteristics, and the records are available for review by internal and external auditors.

- Reported product deficiencies and associated out-of tolerance measuring equipment are submitted for preliminary review or, when appropriate, for assessment by an MRB.

- The customer ensures that calibration system requirements that are delegated to subcontractors are not underspecified or overspecified. Note: The purchaser should be careful not to fall into the trap of duplicating metrology systems management tasks delegated to the subcontractor.

10. *Quality audits.* The factors include:

- The supplier conducts scheduled and unscheduled metrology audits.

- The supplier has a documented metrology audit procedure in place.

- Metrology audits schedules are documented and supported with a tickler file.

- Metrology audits are performed by a second or third party not involved in the processes being audited.

- Top management reviews audit reports and provides proactive recommendations.

- The supplier assures that metrology audits are not performed by the owners of the process.

The costs incurred during the use and maintenance of inspection, measuring, and test instruments associated with a noncomplex, noncritical product design such as an off-the-shelf item are minimal compared with the costs that are required to produce higher-level complex, critical items. Areas that present opportunities to reduce costs include:

- Rental costs for specialized, cost-effective M&TE

- Development of new calibration procedures, processes, work instructions, and techniques

- Trips to subcontractor's facility to assess capabilities and efficiencies regarding the use and calibration of specialized M&TE

- The acquisition of more efficient plant facilities and equipment

ENDNOTES

1. J. Campanella, *Principles of Quality Costs: Principles, Implementation, and Use,* 3rd ed. (Milwaukee: ASQ Quality Press, 1999): 19.
2. U.S. Department of Defense, General Services Administration, and National Aeronautics and Space Administration, *Federal Acquisition Regulation,* part 46, clause 46.203(b) (1995).
3. Ibid., part 46, clause 46.203(c).

8

Self-Assessment of Metrology Systems

The following self-assessment reinforces the information contained in this book. The questions will also help the reader apply calibration system standards, such as ISO 10012:2003, *Measurement management systems—Requirements for measurement processes and measuring equipment.* Specifically, readers who familiarize themselves with the presented issues will be able to:

- Expand their understanding of each element of an adopted calibration system standard.

- Assure that supplies and services delivered to the client are produced with inspection, measuring, and test instruments of known accuracy.

The following questions (Q), answers (A), rationale (R), and references (Ref) are provided to assist instructors whose objective is to share the information with those seeking to improve their skills in the administrative application of metrology systems management. While the term *quiz* implies assessment, the purpose of the questions is to facilitate learning. The primary purpose of this chapter is to help readers become better able to make appropriate day-to-day decisions related to metrology. Readers should also benefit from the rationale that accompanies each answer.

The questions are organized into sections that are relevant to the application of QA requirements for measuring equipment. The sections are as follows:

Code letter	Section
A	Measuring equipment
B	Confirmation system
C	Periodic audit and review of the confirmation system
D	Planning
E	Uncertainty of measurements
F	Documented procedures
G	Records
H	Nonconforming measuring equipment
I	Confirmation labeling
J	Intervals of confirmation
K	Sealing for integrity
L	Use of outside products and services
M	Storage and handling
N	Traceability
O	Cumulative effect of uncertainties
P	Environmental controls
Q	Personnel

A. MEASURING EQUIPMENT[1]

Q1: All inspection equipment and M&TE in a supplier's plant must be calibrated against certified MSs that have a known valid relationship to a national standard.

    a. True

    b. False

A: *True*

R: *Inspection equipment and M&TE can be calibrated by one of, or a combination of, an independent calibration laboratory and the National Institute of Standards and Technology. In-tolerance as well as out-of-tolerance conditions are determined by the review of feedback data furnished by the calibration agency.*
Ref: Chapter 2, p. 37.

Q2: Calibration records are required for each inspection, measuring and test instrument and for each MS.

    a. True

    b. False

A: *True*

R: *Recording of the quality functions is one of the best methods of providing objective quality evidence. Records are made of:*

- *Work accomplished*

- *Compliance with work instructions*

- *Noncompliance with work instructions*

    – *Records that control and maintain the calibration system include item identification, item history, out-of-tolerance conditions, and calibration procedures.*
    Ref: Chapter 2, p. 46

Q3: When the size of a measuring instrument is such that labeling or coding cannot be used, a supplier can include a notation regarding this condition in the written calibration procedure.

    a. True

    b. False

A: *True*

R: *When it is impractical to attach a label to an instrument, it can be attached to the instrument's container.*
Ref: Chapter 2, p. 46

Q4: Production tooling used for inspection purposes is not required to be calibrated because it is used by production personnel and not used by QA personnel.

    a. True

    b. False

A: *False*

R: *Calibration procedures provide metrology personnel with a detailed description of how to perform calibrations for each inspection, measuring, and testing device, including production tooling used for inspection and acceptance purposes.*
Ref: Chapter 5, p. 84

Q5: Certification or reports from other than the NIST shall attest to the fact that the standards used in obtaining the results have been compared with a national standard:

    a. At planned intervals

    b. At least once a year

    c. To the extent necessary

A: *At planned intervals*

R: *Certifications furnished by an independent calibration laboratory should show that the standards used to calibrate its client's measuring instruments have a higher-level accuracy ratio (usually at least 10 times greater than the calibrated instrument). The certificate should also show the date that the master standard was calibrated, the date the transfer standard was calibrated (if appropriate), and the planned date for recalibration.*
Ref: Chapter 2, Figure 2.17, p. 39, and chapter 6, p. 106

Q6: Standards used by a supplier for controlling the accuracy of M&TE and the M&TE that is used for controlling product quality shall have capabilities for:

    a. Accuracy, stability, and range required

    b. Accuracy, precision, and stability required

    c. Stability, purpose, and degree of usage

    d. Accuracy, stability, range, and resolution

A: *Accuracy, stability, range, and resolution*

R: *Standards used by an independent calibration laboratory to calibrate a supplier's standards shall have the accuracy, stability, range, and resolution to ensure that required measurement areas of acceptance are maintained.*
Ref: Chapter 6, p. 105

Q7: Measuring equipment is calibrated to determine and ensure its accuracy.

    a. True

    b. False

A: *True*

R: *The selection of measuring and test equipment begins with knowing the product tolerance of items produced and the accuracy requirements of the related M&TE.*
Ref: Chapter 2, p. 29

Q8: An inventory record for inactive measuring instruments does not have to be established and maintained by the producers of products and services.

    a. True

    b. False

A: *False*

R: *An inventory of all active and inactive measuring instruments, consisting of the following information, is usually located in a separate calibration procedures manual:*

- *Instrument nomenclature*
- *Instrument identification number*
- *Instrument description and use*
- *Nominal value*
- *Accuracy of certified value*
- *Source of calibration*
- *Standard procedures*
- *Instrument manufacturer's written instructions*
- *Company-prepared instructions*
- *Calibration procedure number*

Ref: Chapter 6, p. 102–3

Q9: An instrument cannot be calibrated on one of its usable ranges. The supplier states that the uncalibrated range is not required to be used in the fulfillment of its contractual obligation. A review of associated contracts confirms this requirement. The instrument is required to be labeled to indicate the uncalibrated range.

    a. True

    b. False

A: *True*

R: *Limited-use M&TE should be identified as such: information about the instrument's range should be included.*
Ref: Chapter 2, p. 46

Q10. Measurement confidence can be achieved only through the use of instruments of known accuracy.

a. True

b. False

A: *True*

R: *Accuracy requirements of M&TE are imperative to the corrective-action process aimed at the causes of nonconforming products. In addition, process capability techniques cannot be used to full advantage unless the M&TE and related measurements are reliable.*
Ref: Chapter 2, p. 1

Q11: Requirements of the ISO 10012:2003 standard take the place of other contract quality requirements.

a. True

b. False

A: *False.*

R: *This international standard is not intended to be used as a requisite for demonstrating conformance with ISO 9001, ISO 14001, or any other standard. Interested parties can agree to use this international standard as an input for satisfying measurement management system requirements in certification activities*
Ref: ISO 10012:2003, clause 1

Q12: Calibration is the comparison of two measuring standards or instruments to detect variations in accuracy.

a. True

b. False

A: *True*

R: *Calibration is a set of operations that establish, under specified conditions, the relationship between values indicated by a measuring instrument or measuring system, or values represented by a material measure or a reference material, and corresponding values of a quantity realized by a reference standard.*
Ref: Glossary, p. 199

Q13: What kind of accuracy does a standard or general-purpose instrument have against other standards or instruments that are being calibrated?

    a. Known accuracy

    b. Unknown accuracy

    c. a and b

A: *Known accuracy*

R: *The selection of required M&TE begins with knowing the product tolerance of items produced and the accuracy requirements that relate to M&TE.*
Ref: Chapter 2, p. 29

Q14: General-purpose M&TE is used to check for which of the following?

    a. Transfer standards

    b. Items

    c. All of the above

A: *Items*

R: *M&TE that is used to verify that supplies conform to contract quality requirements should be adequately maintained and controlled in accordance with specified requirements.*
Ref: Chapter 7, p. 135

Q15: M&TE is used to check compliance with specifications.

    a. True

    b. False

A: *True*

R: *A specification is a document that states requirements.*
Ref: Glossary, p. 203

Q16: Reference conditions generally specify "reference values" for the influence quantities affecting the measuring instrument.

   a. True

   b. False

A: *True*

R: *Reference conditions: Conditions of use for a measuring instrument prescribed for performance testing, or to ensure valid intercomparison of results of measurements*
Ref: ISO 10012:1992, clause 3.13

Q17: Instrument standards serve as intermediates between the higher-accuracy standards and lower-accuracy standards.

   a. True

   b. False

A: *True*

R: *The accuracy of M&TE and MSs must be verified with higher-level standards if the integrity of production processes is to be maintained.*
Ref: Chapter 1, p. 11

Q18: Reference materials serve as intermediaries between the higher-accuracy standards and general-purpose measuring instruments.

   a. True

   b. False

A: *True*

R: *The technician must assure that accuracy ratios, between M&TE and the product tolerance and between the MS and the M&TE, are adequate for the purpose intended. A ratio greater than 4:1 is acceptable. A ratio of 10:1 or greater, however, is recommended whenever possible. When measurements fall within an area of uncertainty, a decision must be made as to its impact on out-of-tolerance conditions.*
Ref: Chapter 2, p. 34

Q19: A supplier is required to provide its own M&TE to its client for source inspection requirements.

    a. True

    b. False

A: *False*

R: *The responsibility for operating M&TE is delegated to the supplier's metrology specialists or an independent calibration laboratory. The client might become involved in this operation if a concurrent calibration agreement is a specified component in a statement of work.*
Ref: Chapter 2, p. 19–20

Q20: The client is required to operate the supplier's M&TE independently.

    a. True

    b. False

A: *False*

R: *Unless otherwise specified in a contract, the accuracy of all inspection, measuring, and test instruments used to inspect and test products and services is calibrated by the supplier of the products and services, with higher-level standards of known accuracy.*
Ref: Chapter 6, p. 102

Q21: The client is required to independently verify the accuracy and condition of the M&TE that the supplier uses.

    a. True

    b. False

A: *False*

R: *A supplier substantiates the accuracy and condition of its M&TE by furnishing objective evidence to its client when fulfilling a contractual obligation or during a metrology audit.*
Ref: Chapter 1, p. 10

Q22: Accuracy requirements are verified with higher-level accuracy standards that have an accuracy ratio of 4:1 or higher.

    a. True

    b. False

A: *True*

R: *The accuracy of M&TE is verified against a certified MS, usually with an accuracy ratio between 4:1 and 10:1.*
Ref: Chapter 7, p. 135

Q23: Measuring instruments must be calibrated to their full capability.

    a. True

    b. False

A: *False*

R: *Not necessarily. Recorded information must include any limitation in use. Limited-use M&TE should be identified as such; information about the instrument's range should be included.*
Ref: Chapter 2, p. 46

Q24: Production tooling used as a medium for acceptance inspection requires only an initial calibration.

    a. True

    b. False

A: *False*

R: *M&TE that is used to verify that supplies conform to contract quality requirements should be adequately maintained and controlled in accordance with specified requirements.*
Ref: Chapter 7, p. 135

Q25: Suppose a test instrument that has an accuracy of one percent will be calibrated against a standard that has an accuracy of 0.5 percent. What is the calibration accuracy ratio?

    a. 0.2:1

    b. 2:1

    c. 2.5:1

A: *2:1*

R: *A 2:1 accuracy ratio provides a 50 percent area of acceptance and a 50 percent area of uncertainty.*
Ref: Chapter 2, Table 2.1, p. 33

B. CONFIRMATION SYSTEM[2]

Q1: Suppliers having ISO 10012:2003 specified in contracts establish a calibration system to ensure that products presented for acceptance conform to technical requirements.

a. True

b. False

A: *True*

R: *The supplier as well as the customer's QA representative can complete their assigned functions by understanding and agreeing upon the type of calibration system required.*
Ref: Chapter 1, p. 7

Q2: The supplier does not need to have a written description of his calibration system, provided that its product conforms to contractual requirements.

a. True

b. False

A: *False*

R: *To ensure uniformity of understanding and to ensure continuity of satisfactory operations when personnel changes occur, all proposed or existing calibration procedures should be documented. Without written guides, policy and procedural questions are bound to arise and variations in practice that occur will result in confusion and uncertainty.*
Ref: Chapter 1, p. 7

Q3: Suppliers of products and services that have adopted ISO 10012:2003 as their metrology standard are required to coordinate it with ANSI/ISO/ASQ Q9001-2000.

a. True

b. False

A: *False*

R: *ISO 10012:2003 is not intended to be used as a requisite for demonstrating conformance with ISO 9001 or any other standard. Interested parties can use this international standard as an input for satisfying measurement management system requirements in calibration activities*

Q4:   The supplier shall evaluate the adequacy of its ISO 10012:2003 calibration system based on out-of-tolerance data generated from the calibration of M&TE.

    a.   True

    b.   False

A: *True*

R: *In-tolerance as well as out-of-tolerance conditions are determined by the review of feedback data furnished by calibration agencies.*
Ref: Chapter 2, p. 37–42

Q5:   Preparation and development of a calibration system in accordance with the ISO 10012:2003 standard is required when a contract requires the application of an ANSI/ISO/ASQ Q9001-2000 quality system.

    a.   True

    b.   False

A: *False*

R: *The application of ISO 10012:2003 is not listed in the ANSI/ISO/ASQ Q9001-2000 standard's normative references clause.*
Ref: ANSI/ISO/ASQ Q9001-2000, clause 2

Q6:   One of the critical elements of a quality system is the preparation of an abstract of contract requirements that clearly describe a statement of work.

    a.   True

    b.   False

A: *True*

R: *Each abstract or equivalent method of summarizing contract quality requirements, particularly for new and different product designs, should be reviewed in depth to assure that technical requirements are understood by the metrology manager and his or her staff of specialists.*
Ref: Chapter 5, p. 79

Q7: The calibration system is designed to provide adequate accuracy in the use of inspection equipment and M&TE.

   a. True

   b. False

A: *True*

R: *The selection and application of an appropriate calibration system standard is based on a supplier's own initiative in anticipation of contracts that specify a requirement for the establishment and maintenance of an acceptable calibration system.*
Ref: Chapter 6, p. 97

Q8: The application of a calibration system only pertains to M&TE used in a supplier's plant.

   a. True

   b. False

A: *False*

R: *A supplier's responsibility does not end with in-plant actions. A supplier is also responsible for the accuracy of the measurements and calibration functions performed by outside sources, such as an independent calibration laboratory or a subcontractor's plant.*
Ref: Chapter 1, p. 12

Q9: Early detection of deficiencies is one way that the calibration system helps prevent instrument inaccuracies.

   a. True

   b. False

A: *True*

R: *The calibration system should provide for the prevention of errors outside the specified limits of permissible error by promptly detecting deficiencies and implementing timely corrective action. The confirmation system shall take full account of all relevant data, including that available from any statistical process control system operated by the supplier. Ref: Chapter 3, p. 49*

Q10: Timely and positive corrective action is another way a calibration system provides for the prevention of instrument inaccuracy.

   a. True

   b. False

A: *True*

R: *Timely and positive corrective action is achieved when:*

   • *A documented corrective-action procedure is in place and causes of deficiencies attributed to out-of-tolerance M&TE are eliminated.*

   • *The prime contractor ensures that its subcontractors recalibrate M&TE that is found to be out of tolerance.*

   Ref: Chapter 7, p. 136

Q11: Calibration results are reviewed to ensure the adequacy of a metrology system.

   a. True

   b. False

A: *True*

R: *Feedback data are reviewed and analyzed by the metrology manager or a designated representative at the time of calibration or shortly thereafter to determine the adequacy of the calibration system and equipment reliability. Ref: Chapter 2, p. 40*

Q12: Which requirement of the ISO 10012:2003 standard must be addressed by the written description of a supplier's calibration system?

   a. Contract quality requirements

   b. Quality plan

   c. Each requirement of the standard

A: *Each requirement of the standard*

R: *Several standards set requirements for the establishment, implementation, and continuous control of the accuracy of inspection, measuring, and test instruments. These standards specify criteria that, when met, will be compatible to both the customer and supplier.*
Ref: Chapter 2, p. 16

Q13: A supplier is automatically required to follow later amendments or revisions to a calibration system standard.

   a. True

   b. False

A: *False*

R: *Revisions, additions, and deletions to a specified calibration system are authorized when approved by a contract change notice.*
Ref: Chapter 1, p. 13

Q14: A client does not have to provide the supplier with a written notification about the use of a revised standard or specification.

   a. True

   b. False

A: *False*

R: *Without written guides, policy and procedural questions are bound to arise and variations in practices will result in confusion and uncertainty.*
Ref: Chapter 1, p. 7

C. PERIODIC AUDIT AND REVIEW OF THE CONFIRMATION SYSTEM[3]

Q1: Internal audits are conducted to ensure that contract quality requirements have been met.

    a. True

    b. False

A: *True*

R: *Internal audits are conducted to verify that contract-related policies, procedures, and processes are being followed.*
Ref: Chapter 3, p. 49

Q2: Metrology audits should be conducted by an experienced QA specialist, preferably by a certified auditor.

    a. True

    b. False

A: *True*

R: *Metrology audits should be performed by certified or experienced QA specialists who do not have specific responsibilities in the area being audited.*
Ref: Chapter 3, p. 49

Q3: Metrology audits may be carried out by

    a. A supplier's qualified specialist

    b. An outside consultant

    c. A certified auditor

    d. All of the above

A: *All of the above*

R: *If an audit is complex in nature, it can be delegated to a team of specialists consisting of the QA director, a quality engineer, a metrology manager, and a calibration technician.*
Ref: Chapter 3, p. 50

Q4: Audit responsibilities may be delegated to a qualified individual and not to a team of metrology specialists.

    a. True

    b. False

A: *True*

R: *If an audit is complex in nature, it can be delegated to a team of specialists consisting of the QA director, a quality engineer, a metrology manager, and a calibration technician. However, noncomplex audits are usually performed by one person.*
Ref: Chapter 3, p. 50

Q5: External metrology audits are conducted by the supplier.

    a. True

    b. False

A: *True*

R: *External metrology audits are conducted at a time when a prime contractor (supplier) decides to delegate some or all of the metrology functions to an independent calibration laboratory.*
Ref: Chapter 3, p. 50

Q6: A "desk audit" precedes the application of an on-site audit.

    a. True

    b. False

A: *True*

R: *An audit begins with a "desk review" of established policies and procedures, followed by the verification of those policies and procedures at the applicable calibration areas and inspection stations.*
Ref: Chapter 3, p. 50

Q7: If it is determined at the time of a scheduled audit that the policies and procedures are inadequate, the audit should be immediately terminated.

    a. True

    b. False

A: *False*

R: *Not necessarily. If documented policies and procedures are unavailable at the time of a scheduled audit or if they are considered inadequate, a report of these findings should be brought to the attention of the responsible department supervisor. The audit team must then terminate the calibration audit but continue to perform an audit of operations (when this action is determined by the team leader to be in the best interest of the QA process). The calibration audit must be rescheduled after the required documentation is in place and put into operation.*
Ref: Chapter 3, p. 50

Q8:   What factors should be considered when preparing a checklist for each element of a calibration system that is to be audited?

  a.   Name of the element to be evaluated

  b.   Characteristics to be evaluated

  c.   Pertinent section and paragraph of the documented system to be evaluated

  d.   Adequacy or inadequacy of systems description

  e.   Adequacy or inadequacy of systems application

  f.   All of the above

A: *All of the above*

R: *An audit checklist should be prepared in advance of the actual audit for each element of the system that is to be audited. This checklist should address these five topics.*
Ref: Chapter 3, p. 51

Q9:   Suppliers who have a metrology audit system in place are only required to conduct *scheduled* audits.

  a.   True

  b.   False

A: *False*

R: *Suppliers conduct scheduled as well as unscheduled audits.*
Ref: Chapter 7, p. 138

Q10: When multiple deficiencies become evident, a major milestone chart should be implemented to monitor the corrective-action process.

    a. True

    b. False

A: *True*

R: *At a minimum, the milestone chart should distribute the audit findings and list the nonconformances found and the anticipated dates of corrective action. If more than 30 days are required to accomplish satisfactory corrective action, arrangements should be made for mutually agreed-upon progress reports. A progress report should be shown on a milestone schedule and supported with a cover letter.*
Ref: Chapter 3, p. 63

Q11: Metrology audits are performed by:

    a. First party

    b. Second party

    c. Third party

    d. b & c

    e. All of the above

A: *Second party, third party*

R: *Metrology audits are performed by a second or third party that is not involved in the process being audited.*
Ref: Chapter 7, p. 138

Q12: An auditor must select only those elements of a calibration system and those related factors that can be traceable to active documents.

    a. True

    b. False

A: *True*

R: *When conducting a metrology audit, caution must be taken to select only those elements of a calibration system and their related factors that can be traceable to active documents. These active documents include policies, procedures, and processes.*
       Ref: Chapter 3, p. 64

Q13:   Auditors should immediately notify the recipient of an audit about any nonconforming processes they find.

   a. True

   b. False

A: *True*

R: *If nonconforming conditions are in evidence, observations should be clearly stated in the audit report. In addition, the report should explain how each deficiency relates to contract quality requirements, the calibration system description, calibration procedure, and/or work instructions.*
       Ref: Chapter 3, p. 63

Q14:   Inspection and testing records that are traceable to M&TE should be a component of an audit checklist.

   a. True

   b. False

A: *True*

R: *Traceability of the M&TE that is used to check product characteristics should be readily available for review by internal and external auditors.*
       Ref: Chapter 7, p. 137

Q15:   A small organization can elect to delegate a calibration audit to a technician who is the owner of a calibration process.

   a. True

   b. False

A: *False*

R: *Metrology audits are performed by a second or third party and not by someone who is directly involved in the process being audited.*
       Ref: Chapter 7, p. 138

D. PLANNING[4]

Q1: The planning process begins with a prompt review of a solicitation, open contracts, and a related technical data package.

   a. True

   b. False

A: *True*

R: *Failure to review, identify, and summarize contract quality and product design requirements; failure to assure there is a clear understanding of technical requirements; or the failure to consider personnel, equipment, and facility requirements might jeopardize contract performance and delivery schedules, which usually leads to unanticipated costs when producing a product or service.*
   Ref: Chapter 1, p. 8

Q2: When the authorized customer and supplier representatives have different opinions about the application of contract quality requirements, what is the next course of action?

   a. Notify the chairman of the MRB.

   b. Conduct a post-award conference between authorized customer and supplier QA representatives.

   c. Refer the condition to the supplier's customer complaint monitor.

A: *Conduct a post-award conference between authorized customer and supplier QA representatives.*

R: *If ambiguity or differences of opinion exist between the customer and supplier concerning the application of contract requirements, and if clarification cannot be accomplished via telephone or correspondence, then a post-award orientation conference between key customer and supplier QA representatives might be required.*
   Ref: Chapter 2, p. 21

Q3: A post-award orientation conference is convened to ensure that there is a clear understanding of contract quality requirements.

   a. True

   b. False

A: *True*

R: *A post-award conference aids both customer and supplier to achieve a mutual understanding of all contract requirements and to identify and resolve potential problems.*
Ref: Chapter 2, p. 21

Q4: A master requirements list is a recommended method for communicating metrology requirements.

   a. True

   b. False

A: *True*

R: *A master requirements list is prepared for each product or assembly. It requires modification only when there are significant changes to the product design or other contract quality requirements.*
Ref: Chapter 2, p. 21

Q5: There are three important factors that must be addressed when planning for the application of a calibration system. Which of the following is *not* one of those factors?

   a. The identification of the tightest product tolerances allowed for the products and services offered

   b. The identification of out-of-service measuring instruments

   c. The types of calibration equipment that will be needed to check the product and M&TE

   d. The need to solicit the services of an independent calibration laboratory to perform all or a part of the calibration processes

A: *The identification of out-of-service measuring instruments*

R: *When planning a calibration system, three factors must be addressed:*

   • *The identification of the tightest product tolerances allowed for the products and services offered. The satisfactory identification and control of the tightest product tolerance will provide positive indications that other products with looser tolerances will be adequately controlled.*

- *The types of calibration equipment that will be needed to check the product and M&TE. Due consideration should be given to the accuracy level of the M&TE and MSs that are required to check the product. A high accuracy ratio between a comparator and the item being checked will reduce potential measurement error.*

- *The need to solicit the services of an independent calibration laboratory to perform all or a part of the calibration processes. If the suggested source is one with unknown calibration capabilities, the supplier must evaluate the capabilities of those potential outside sources prior to issuing a purchase order for required services.*

Ref: Chapter 1, p. 13–14

Q6: There are three factors that should be considered when establishing a metrology-related quality plan. Which of the following is *not* one of those factors?

- a. Direct relationship between a client and a supplier's subcontractor

- b. Requirements for special inspection and test equipment, tooling, and skills.

- c. Tailored specification requirements that have a direct bearing on the selection of special inspection and test equipment.

- d. Procedures for comparing new contract or purchase order requirements with previously prepared metrology procedures and processes.

A: *Direct relationship between a client and a supplier's subcontractor.*

R: *The quality plan should be capable of addressing:*

- *All of the technical requirements specified in a contractual agreement between two parties or in a system for handling exceptions*

- *Requirements for special inspection and test equipment, tooling, and skills*

- *Tailored specification requirements that have a direct bearing on the selection of special inspection and test equipment*

- *Procedures for comparing new contracts or purchase order requirements with previously prepared metrology procedures and processes and for making changes when appropriate*

Ref: Chapter 7, p. 133

Q7: What other factors should be considered when establishing a quality plan?

a. The acquisition of new facilities and measuring equipment

b. Method of recording calibration measurements

c. Environmental conditions under which calibration measurements are taken

d. All of the above

A: *All of the above*

R: *The quality plan should address:*

- *The need for acquiring new facilities and inspection measuring and test equipment*

- *The method for recording calibration measurements (variable and attribute data)*

- *The acceptable environmental conditions under which calibration measurements are taken and the method for identifying these conditions.*

Ref: Chapter 7, p. 133

Q8: Calibration systems planning is accomplished by the:

a. QA director

b. Metrology manager

c. Technician

d. All of the above

A: *All of the above*

R: *Calibration systems planning is accomplished by the QA director, the metrology manager, and their staff of technicians.*
Ref: Chapter 6, p. 104

E. UNCERTAINTY OF MEASUREMENTS[5]

Q1: When determining the adequacy of MS and M&TE, the metrology technician monitors potential measurement error, and the area of uncertainty that exists on every side of every reading. The technician also reduces the acceptable range of an acceptable reading by the prescribed tolerance of the measuring device (comparator).

    a. True

    b. False

A: *True*

R: *The technician allows for:*

- *The limitations inherent in the construction of the M&TE*

- *The environmental conditions under which measurements are made*

- *The different ways people use and read measuring equipment*

Ref: Chapter 2, p. 32

Q2: An area of uncertainty between an MS and M&TE that is greater than 10 percent is better than one that is less than 10 percent.

    a. True

    b. False

A: *False*

R: *An area of uncertainty that is greater that 10 percent reduces an area of acceptance.*
Ref: Chapter 2, Table 2.2, p. 37

Q3: The collective area of uncertainty of measurement standards shall not exceed 25 percent.

    a. True

    b. False

A: *True*

R: *Unless otherwise specified in contract requirements, the collective uncertainty of the measurement standards shall not exceed 25 percent of the acceptable tolerance for each characteristic being calibrated. An area of uncertainty found to be greater that 25 percent will usually require an investigation to determine the adequacy of established calibration procedures as well as the quality status of products and services produced.*
Ref: Chapter 2, p. 32 and chapter 6, p. 108

Q4: When an accuracy ratio between two measuring devices is 1:1, what is the percentage of uncertainty?

   a. 20 percent

   b. 50 percent

   c. 100 percent

A: *100 percent*

R: *A 1:1 accuracy ratio will reflect a 100 percent area of uncertainty. Therefore, all measurements that fall within an item's tolerance range will land in an area of uncertainty.*
Ref: Chapter 2, p. 32 and Table 2.2, p. 37

Q5: A 1:1 accuracy ratio between a measuring instrument and the item being checked may be considered acceptable.

   a. True

   b. False

A: *True*

R: *It is acceptable when state-of-the-art limitations preclude the use of accuracy ratios greater than 1:1.*
Ref: Chapter 2, p. 32

Q6: Knowledgeable suppliers recognize that a 10:1 or higher-level accuracy ratio between an MS and M&TE is generally recommended.

   a. True

   b. False

A: *True*

R: *These suppliers recognize that a 10:1 accuracy level between MSs and working M&TE is an important element of a calibration. The use of a ratio of 10:1 or higher will provide greater measurement confidence and will reduce potential measurement error.*
Ref: Chapter 7, p. 135 and chapter 2, p. 34

Q7: A product characteristic is one inch +/– 0.005 inch. It is inspected with a measuring device with an accuracy of 0.001 inch. What is the area of uncertainty?

    a. 25 percent

    b. 20 percent

    c. 33 percent

A: *20 percent*

R: *The area of uncertainty is one-fifth of the accuracy ratio.*
Ref: Chapter 2, Table 2.2, p. 37

F. DOCUMENTED PROCEDURES[6]

Q1: Written calibration procedures for M&TE are not required, provided the technician is capable of performing calibrations without a procedure.

    a. True

    b. False

A: *False*

R: *The supplier shall designate and use documented procedures for all M&TE and MSs. There are three main sources of calibration procedures:*

    1. Procedures compiled by the product manufacturer

    2. Published standards

    3. Instrument manufacturer's recommended calibration procedures

Ref: Chapter 2, p. 26

Q2: Suppliers may use the instrument manufacturer's instructions word for word in their written calibration procedures.

    a. True

    b. False

A: *True*

R: *An instrument manufacturer's calibration procedure may be used word for word if the calibrated instrument is used over its entire range. However, the instrument manufacturer's instructions will be complete, which means the supplier would be documenting the full calibration procedure. If the instrument is not required to be used over its entire range, full calibration is not necessary or economical.*
Ref: Chapter 2, p. 29

Q3: A supplier's procedure states that some inspection, measuring, and test instruments are to be calibrated before use. The procedure also states that the instruments falling within this category should be labeled as such. Is the supplier required to control and document each use?

    a. Yes

    b. No

A: *Yes*

R: *Calibrations can be accomplished on an established frequency or prior to use. When there is sporadic production, the prior-to-use method is recommended. The results of all calibrated measuring instruments are documented.*

There are no restrictions placed on metrology managers as to what methodology is used to establish an interval of calibration that satisfactorily meets a reliability target or how to adjust a calibration interval if the target is not being met. Specific intervals of calibration for inspection equipment, M&TE, and MSs can be established contractually by a calibration laboratory that is located in the manufacturer's facility or by an independent laboratory. Whatever the source, the supplier of the metrology service must demonstrate that each instrument is calibrated and traceable to objective quality evidence.
Ref: Chapter 2, p. 23 and chapter 7, p. 127

Q4: The supplier's procedure defines a significant out-of-tolerance condition as a condition that has an adverse effect on product quality, as determined by a quality engineer.

    a. True

    b. False

A: *False*

R: *A significant out-of-tolerance condition occurs when an instrument's accuracy ratio deteriorates to less than 2:1. Ref: Chapter 2, p. 42*

Q5: Written calibration procedures shall state the MS required for calibration and the required accuracy of the standard that will be used for calibration.

    a. True

    b. False

A: *True*

R: *The primary purpose of preparing calibration procedures is to provide metrology personnel with a detailed description of how to perform calibrations of each inspection, measuring, and testing device that is used within the system. The procedures identify the standards that will be used to verify the accuracy of the calibrated working instruments. In addition to the step-by-step calibration procedure, calibration instructions should address:*

- *The accuracy tolerance of calibrated instruments*

- *The area of uncertainty of the characteristic being calibrated*

- *The accuracy ratio between the measurement standard and the characteristic being calibrated*

Ref: Chapter 5, p. 84

Q6: Written calibration procedures are not required when the technician performing the calibration designed and built the equipment.

    a. True

    b. False

A: *False*

R: *The QC manager or a designated representative are responsible for the content of a calibration procedure.*
Ref: Chapter 2, p. 20

Q7: The supplier's written calibration system shall include a list of reference and transfer standards

   a. True

   b. False

A: *True*

R: *An inventory of all reference and transfer standards as well as general-purpose instruments shall be maintained and updated when appropriate.*
Ref: Chapter 6, p. 102

Q8: A published standard is considered an acceptable calibration procedure.

   a. True

   b. False

A: *True*

R: *A compilation of published standards is available to participating members from GIDEP.*
Ref: Chapter 2, p. 27

Q9: An instrument manufacturer's written instructions is another source of acceptable calibration procedures.

   a. True

   b. False

A: *True*

R: *The instrument manufacturer's recommended calibration procedures are normally furnished with the purchased instrument. Occasionally, these procedures might have to be ordered under separate cover.*
Ref: Chapter 2, p. 29

Q10: A calibration procedure must specify the *accuracy* of general-purpose instruments and MSs.

a. True

b. False

A: *True*

R: *A product manufacturer's calibration procedures should address instrument accuracy requirements. The procedures must be upgraded when conditions warrant this action.*
Ref: Chapter 2, p. 27

Q11: Documented procedures shall ensure that active as well as inactive documents are available at working product and service verification stations.

a. True

b. False

A: *False*

R: *Timely documentation of calibration requirements, when coordinated with inspection and testing requirements, will preclude the inadvertent omission of contract quality requirements and, at the same time, enhance the quality expectations the customer. Obsolete documents should always be removed from points of issue and use.*
Ref: Chapter 1, p. 14

Q12: Documented metrology data is reviewed for reliability and improvement.

a. As determined by the calibration technician

b. As determined by the contract administrator

c. On a regularly scheduled basis

A: *On a regularly scheduled basis*

R: *Metrology data is documented and reviewed by management for reliability and improvement on a regularly scheduled basis.*
Ref: Chapter 7, p. 134

Q13: Calibration data must be reviewed and analyzed.

   a. True

   b. False

A: *True*

R: *Documented calibration inspection records are reviewed and analyzed to identify problem areas.*
Ref: Chapter 7, p. 134

Q14: The effective date of contract change notices associated with metrology requirements shall be identified.

   a. True

   b. False

A: *True*

R: *The control of design changes that impact the metrology system is documented and the effective date of contract change notices associated with metrology requirements is identified.*
Ref: Chapter 7, p. 134

Q15: Procedures for documenting the adequacy of technical documents associated with a metrology system are not required.

   a. True

   b. False

A: *False*

R: *QA personnel must have ready access to an abstract of contract requirements and active documents. If policy and procedures are to be satisfactorily maintained, QA personnel must know of changes in technical requirements and determine the impact that those changes have on established calibration policies and procedures.*
Ref: Chapter 2, p. 47

G. RECORDS[7]

Q1: Calibration records are required for each inspection, measuring, and test instrument and each MS.

    a. True

    b. False

A: *True*

R: *A calibration record should identify:*

- *Instrument nomenclature*
- *Model number*
- *Identification number*
- *Accuracy of the instrument*
- *Procedure number*
- *Resolution value*
- *Calibration frequency*
- *Characteristic identification*
- *Work performance*
- *Characteristic identification*
- *Measured value*

Ref: Chapter 6, p. 110

Q2: The written description need not include controls of production tooling used for inspection and acceptance.

    a. True

    b. False

A: *False*

R: *If a calibration system is to be cost-effective, it must provide satisfactory provisions for maintaining the accuracy of all M&TE and MSs that are used in house as well as by subcontractors. Ref: Chapter 1, p. 11*

Q3: Individual calibration records are required only for MSs and not for inspection equipment and M&TE.

    a. True

    b. False

A: *False*

R: *The accuracy and history of inspection equipment and M&TE is documented after being verified against a certified primary or secondary MS.*
Ref: Chapter 7, p. 135

Q4: The supplier shall provide objective evidence in the form of records, reports, certifications, procedures, and evidence of accuracy conformance to the client upon request.

    a. True

    b. False

A: *True*

R: *The process of establishing objective quality evidence regarding calibration capability that will meet the interests of a product manufacturer or an independent calibration laboratory as well as meet the expectations of customers starts with contract quality requirements that are clearly communicated from the purchaser to the supplier and from the supplier to the metrology department.*
Ref: Chapter 5, p. 91

Q5: Calibration records are required for each general-purpose instrument and MS.

    a. True

    b. False

A: *True*

R: *The absence of objective records will impede the objectives of good management. The collection, review, and analysis of records are necessary to measure the effectiveness of a supplier's calibration system as well as to indicate the supplier's calibration capabilities.*
Ref: Chapter 1, p. 12

Q6: Recording quality management functioning is one of the best methods for providing objective quality evidence.

    a. True

    b. False

A: *True*

R: *Records shall be made available for: work accomplished, compliance with work instructions, and noncompliance with work instructions.*
Ref: Chapter 2, p. 46

Q7: Instrument-related certificates and reports that are received from an outside source are examined and validated by the purchasing department.

    a. True

    b. False

A: *False*

R: *The metrology manager or a designated representative shall validate certificates and reports associated with a calibrated instrument by applying his or her signature to the certificate or report before it is filed.*
Ref: Chapter 6, p. 121

Q8: Corrective action associated with the receipt of certificates or reports that are found to be nonconforming is the responsibility of the:

    a. QA director

    b. Contract administrator

    c. Purchasing director

    d. All of the above

A: *Purchasing director*

R: *Files are routed to the purchasing director via the QA director when a certificate or report is found to be nonconforming.*
Ref: Chapter 6, p. 121

Q9: The retention time of files is predetermined by authorized customer and supplier representatives.

   a. True

   b. False

A: *True*

R: *A supplier's files are held at least three years or as many years as are specified in a contractual agreement.*
     Ref: Chapter 6, p. 121

H. NONCONFORMING MEASURING EQUIPMENT[8]

Q1: Inspection, measuring, and test instruments found to be out of tolerance at the end of a calibration cycle could indicate several problems. If an out-of-tolerance instrument is found, the best course of action taken by a supplier or an independent calibration laboratory is to:

   a. Disagree since the product might have been shipped

   b. Disagree because this condition does not happen very often

   c. Review the instrument's effect on product quality by examining the products previously inspected by that instrument

A: *Review the instrument's effect on product quality by examining the products previously inspected by that instrument*

R: *Procedures associated with nonconforming products and services include a requirement for the investigation of the metrology procedures, the measuring equipment that was used to inspect the product, and the related calibration data to determine the impact on products previously produced.*
     Ref: Chapter 7, p. 136

Q2: The supplier keeps track of out-of-tolerance calibrations to:

   a. Know when they occur

   b. Ensure that they have no effect on product quality

   c. Accumulate data on the frequency of occurrences

   d. Have quantitative data available in records

A: *Ensure that they have no effect on product quality*

R: *The calibration technician reports significant out-of-tolerance conditions to the metrology manager and to other department managers who depend on the use of M&TE of known accuracy. Ref: Chapter 5, p. 91*

Q3: Who is responsible for notifying the test equipment user of out–of-tolerance conditions?

    a. The supplier's designated QA representative

    b. The customer

    c. The calibration laboratory

    d. A quality engineer

A: *Calibration laboratory*

R: *When an out-of-tolerance condition prevails, the calibrating agency conducts an investigation to determine:*

    • *The accuracy of the MSs used to calibrate the M&TE*

    • *The adequacy of the M&TE used to check the product*

    • *The adequacy of the calibration intervals*

    • *The quality of products accepted in-house as well as the quality of the products shipped to the customers*

    • *The adequacy of the established calibration procedures*

    Ref: Chapter 2, p. 42

Q4: The supplier is required to notify a client's QA representative when a significant out-of-tolerance condition is discovered for an inspection, measuring, or test instrument.

    a. True

    b. False

A: *False*

R: *Significant out-of-tolerance conditions must be brought to the attention of the supplier's department supervisor(s) for appropriate action. Ref: Chapter 2, p. 42*

Q5: Suppliers of products and services evaluate out-of-tolerance data generated during the calibration process to:

   a. Select qualified calibration sources

   b. Know when out-of-tolerance conditions occur

   c. Establish adequate calibration intervals

   d. Adjust calibration intervals

   e. All of the above

  A: *Establish adequate calibration intervals, adjust calibration intervals*

  R: *Calibration records play an important role in the establishment and adjustment of calibration intervals. The justification of interval adjustment is predicated on data generated during previous calibrations.*
Ref: Chapter 2, p. 24

Q6: What corrective action must be taken when measuring instruments are found to be out of tolerance?

   a. Identify the quality status of products in-house and elsewhere

   b. Determine whether there is a need to adjust calibration intervals

   c. Determine whether there is a need to modify established calibration procedures

   d. Determine the adequacy of the calibration system and equipment reliability

   e. All of the above

  A: *All of the above*

  R: *Feedback data are reviewed and analyzed by the metrology manager or a designated representative to identify out-of-tolerance equipment and prevent the use of that equipment until the reported deficiency has been corrected.*
Ref: Chapter 2, p. 40

Q7: Proposed or existing changes to calibration procedures shall be documented.

    a. True

    b. False

A: *True*

R: *To ensure uniformity of understanding and to ensure continuity of satisfactory operations when personnel changes occur, all proposed or existing calibration procedures should be documented. Ref: Chapter 1, p. 7*

Q8: When an accuracy ratio between a comparator and an item deteriorates to less than 2:1, it is considered a significant out-of-tolerance condition.

    a. True

    b. False

A: *True*

R: *When instrument accuracy deteriorates to less than 2:1, the instrument will have a major impact on the accuracy requirements of MSs and M&TE. It is a condition that will require immediate corrective action. Ref: Chapter 2, p. 42*

Q9: A significant out-of-tolerance condition does not have to be documented and identified.

    a. True

    b. False

A: *False*

R: *Significant out-of-tolerance conditions, which adversely affect product and service quality, shall be documented on a metrology deficiency report form provided for that purpose. Ref: Chapter 6, p. 114*

Q10: When an accuracy ratio between a comparator and an item deteriorates to between 2:1 and 4:1, an instrument is classified as having a significant out-of-tolerance condition.

   a. True

   b. False

A: *False*

R: *When instrument accuracy deteriorates to between 2:1 and 4:1, this out-of-tolerance trend is not considered significant. However, the applicable factors that contribute to this out-of-tolerance trend will have to be investigated.*
Ref: Chapter 2, p. 42

Q11: The desired accuracy ratio between MSs and inspection, measuring, and test instruments should be from 4:1 to 10:1 (or higher).

   a. True

   b. False

A: *True*

R: *When a 4:1 to 10:1 (or higher) accuracy ratio is maintained, the adequacy of MSs and inspection, measuring, and test instruments will be satisfactorily maintained.*
Ref: Chapter 2, p. 42

Q12: Out-of-tolerance measuring equipment is not subject to preliminary review and MRB action.

   a. True

   b. False

A: *False*

R: *Nonconforming M&TE are processed via preliminary review and, when necessary, via an MRB.*
Ref: Chapter 7, p. 136

Q13: Nonconforming products are reworked and reinspected and, when appropriate, associated measuring instruments are recalibrated.

   a. True

   b. False

A: *True*

R: *Nonconforming products are reworked and measuring instruments are repaired using documented procedures that are acceptable to both internal and external customers.*
Ref: Chapter 7, p. 136

Q14: The reason for reporting a significant out-of-tolerance condition is to notify the plant manager that a problem exists within the quality system.

   a. True

   b. False

A: *False*

R: *Significant out-of-tolerance conditions are reported to the metrology manager and, when appropriate, to other department supervisors that depend on the use of M&TE of known accuracy. This report alerts the metrology manager to the problem so that he or she can take immediate corrective action to preclude the acceptance of products using the instrument with questionable accuracy.*
Ref: Chapter 5, p. 91

I. CONFIRMATION[9]

Q1: Measuring instruments are labeled to indicate their calibration status.

   a. True

   b. False

A: *True*

R: *The confirmation status of the M&TE used to inspect and test products and services is identified on labels or tags. Where practical, the following information should be referenced on labels or tags:*

   • *Date of calibration*

   • *Due date for next calibration*

   • *Calibrated by*

- *For limited-use instruments, the instrument's acceptable range*

- *Person responsible for confirmation*

- *Compensating correction factors when appropriate*

Ref: Chapter 6, p. 115–16

Q2: Calibration status is accomplished by the use of tags, labels, or color coding.

  a. True

  b. False

A: *True*

R: *The selected method shall, at a minimum, identify the date, month, and year the instrument was calibrated, as well as the calibration due date.*
Ref: Chapter 2, p. 46

Q3: Calibration labels can be attached to an instrument's container.

  a. True

  b. False

A: *True*

R: *When it is impractical to attach a label to the instrument, it can be attached to the instrument's container.*
Ref: Chapter 2, p. 46

Q4: Limited-use instruments are required to be identified as such.

  a. True

  b. False

A: *True*

R: *Example: If the full range of a pressure gage is from 0–100 pounds per square inch (psi) and the product is required to be checked from 0–50 psi, then the limited use of M&TE shall be identified as such and the range of the instrument shall be identified.*
Ref: Chapter 2, p. 46

Q5: Obsolete and out-of-service instruments can be identified and stored in the same manner as active measuring instruments.

    a. True

    b. False

A: *False*

R: *Obsolete and out-of-service instruments should be identified as such and stored apart from active equipment.*
Ref: Chapter 2, p. 46

Q6: If the size or function of an instrument or MS prohibits the use of labeling, color coding may be employed.

    a. True

    b. False

A: *True*

R: *Color coding can be used instead of labeling when the small size or the functional characteristics of the instrument preclude container marking, labels, or tags. Color coding provides only the year and month that the instrument is due for recalibration.*
Ref: Chapter 6, p. 116

Q7: A supplier's labeling system applies to all measuring instruments.

    a. True

    b. False

A: *True*

R: *An effective system for controlling nonconforming material includes procedures for identification, segregation, and disposition of nonconforming products and metrology services.*
Ref: Chapter 7, p. 136

Q8: A supplier should provide evidence to its client's QA representative that its subcontractors have an adequate labeling system.

    a. True

    b. False

A: *True*

R: *The QA director and the metrology manager support the
purchasing manager when soliciting capable outside calibration
sources. All purchase requisitions are reviewed by the metrology
manager for adequacy and approved by the QA director.
Ref: Chapter 6, p. 118*

J. INTERVALS OF CONFIRMATION[10]

Q1: A measuring instrument may be used beyond an established
calibration interval to meet an emergency condition.

   a. True

   b. False

A: *True.*

R: *A temporary extension of calibration due dates may be authorized
only when a favorable in-tolerance history is in evidence. Unless
otherwise authorized by the customer, no shipments should be
made to the customer until the pertinent measuring equipment
has been found to be in tolerance and the calibration results are
documented on the respective form furnished for this purpose.
Ref: Chapter 2, p. 25*

Q2: A supplier should change calibration intervals when:

   a. Preceding results of calibration indicate no appreciable
changes in equipment stability.

   b. The supplier changes calibration sources for calibrating its
reference standards.

   c. After operating one eight-hour shift daily for a long period,
the supplier is now operating a second eight-hour shift daily
for an indefinite period of time.

A: *After operating one eight-hour shift daily for a long period, the
supplier is now operating a second eight-hour shift daily for an
indefinite period of time.*

R: *Appropriate intervals (usually periodic) are established on the
basis of usage (as well as stability and purpose).
Ref: Chapter 6, p. 117*

Q3: Calibration intervals for inspection, measuring, and test instruments and MSs should be established by a supplier:

    a. Using published schedules

    b. Based on stability, purpose, and usage

A: *Based on stability, purpose, and usage*

R: *Intervals of confirmation of M&TE and MS are assigned and maintained by the metrology manager and his or her staff of calibration technicians.*
Ref: Chapter 6, p. 117

Q4: Calibration intervals may be shortened.

    a. True

    b. False

A: *True*

R: *Intervals of confirmation shall be shortened when the record reflects an unfavorable calibration history.*
Ref: Chapter 6, p. 118

Q5: Calibration intervals may not be lengthened.

    a. True

    b. False

A: *False*

R: *Intervals may be lengthened if the results of previous calibrations provide positive indications that the accuracy of the equipment will not be adversely affected.*
Ref: Chapter 2, p. 24

Q6: A recall system must be established for maintaining the accuracy of MSs, inspection equipment, and M&TE.

    a. True

    b. False

A: *True*

R: *A recall system must be in place to assure that calibrations are performed within specified intervals. The establishment and maintenance of a recall location record ensures that calibration schedules will be met.*
Ref: Chapter 2, p. 24

Q7: M&TE and MSs are calibrated periodically to meet a supplier's needs and interests.

   a. True

   b. False

A: *False*

R: *Measuring equipment should be calibrated as often as necessary to maintain the prescribed accuracy. Calibration may be accomplished on an established frequency or prior to use. When there is sporadic production, the prior-to-use method is recommended. When production is continuous, the establishment of calibration frequencies is recommended.*
Ref: Chapter 2, p. 23

K. SEALING FOR INTEGRITY[11]

Q1: Who is responsible for applying tamper-resistant seals to inspection, measuring, and test instruments and MSs?

   a. Metrology technician

   b. Contract administrator

   c. Plant manager

   d. QA director

   e. Customer's QA representative

   f. All of the above

A: *QA director, customer's QA representative*

R: *The QA director, with support from the customer's QA representative, shall identify instruments that require seals based on their experience regarding how the instruments are used in support of contract quality requirements.*
Ref: Chapter 6, p. 117

Q2: Department supervisors are responsible for the removal of instruments from use when seals are found broken.

a. True

b. False

A: *False*

R: *The calibration technician verifies that instruments are removed from use if the seals are found broken.*
Ref: Chapter 6, p. 117

Q3: Measuring instruments whose seals are broken shall be immediately removed from use.

a. True

b. False

A: *True*

R: *Tamper-resistant seals shall be affixed to operator-accessible adjustments that, if moved, will affect the calibration of the M&TE or MS.*
Ref: Chapter 6, p. 117

L. USE OF OUTSIDE PRODUCTS AND SERVICES[12]

Q1: The supplier is responsible for ensuring that subcontractors have a system that essentially meets the requirements of a specified metrological confirmation system for measuring equipment.

a. True

b. False

A: *True*

R: *A representative from the QC department conducts an on-site assessment of the proposed supplier's QA capabilities before a purchase order is issued for solicited instruments and/or calibration services under the following conditions:*

• *The supplier did not achieve ISO certification and registration status*

- *In the company's files, there is no history to indicate the subcontractor's capabilities*

- *A supplier does not have an established reputation within the industry to indicate acceptable capabilities*

Ref: Chapter 6, p. 119

Q2:   A supplier's responsibility ends with in-plant calibration actions.

  a. True

  b. False

A: *False*

R: *A supplier must ensure the accuracy of all measurements and calibration functions performed by outside sources, such as an independent laboratory or a subcontractor's plant.*
Ref: Chapter 1, p. 12

Q3:   All functions of a calibration system are conducted by a prime contractor.

  a. True

  b. False

A: *False*

R: *Functions of a calibration system are usually performed by a prime contractor. However, there will be situations in which a prime contractor will delegate all or some of its calibration system requirements to a subcontractor.*
Ref: Chapter 1, p. 12

Q4:   The responsibility for managing the metrology system by an outsource facility is divided among the QC manager, quality engineer, calibration technician, and metrology manager.

  a. True

  b. False

A: *False*

R: *Some companies cannot afford the expense associated with a full staff of managers. Under these conditions, all or most of the responsibilities are shared by the QC manager and calibration technician.*
Ref: Chapter 1, p. 13

Q5: The prime contractor is responsible to its customer for those calibration system requirements delegated to its subcontractors.

    a. True

    b. False

A: *True*

R: *A prime contractor (supplier) is responsible to the customer for the calibration system elements delegated to its subcontractor. The subcontractor, in turn, is responsible to its prime contractor regarding specific contract requirements delegated to it.*
Ref: Chapter 1, p. 13

Q6: Calibration system requirements that are delegated to a subcontractor shall be specifically related to contract quality requirements.

    a. True

    b. False

A: *True*

R: *Calibration system requirements that are delegated to a subcontractor shall not be underspecified or overspecified. The purchaser should be careful not to fall into the trap of duplicating metrology systems management requirements delegated to the subcontractor.*
Ref: Chapter 7, p. 138

Q7: A supplier shall ensure that calibration services provided by an outside source are supported with a report, certificate, or data sheet under which calibrations to reference standards were obtained.

    a. True

    b. False

A: *True*

R: *In-tolerance conditions as well as out-of-tolerance conditions are determined by the review of feedback data provided by the calibration agency. Examples of the forms that are used by the calibration agency to record calibration data are found in Figures 2.16, 2.17, and 2.18.*
Ref: Chapter 2, p. 37

Q8: Supplier of products and services does not have to obtain quality evidence regarding the traceability of their working standards to a national or international standard.

a. True

b. False

A: *False*

R: *The metrology manager ensures that the purchase orders will include in the statement of work that company standards will be calibrated with higher-level standards with an accuracy ratio of at least 10 times better than the instrument being calibrated and with an area of uncertainty of no greater than 10 percent. The statement of work will also include requirements for the laboratory to furnish a certified calibration report showing a list of actual measurements and the total area (values) of uncertainty. Ref: Chapter 6, p. 106*

M. STORAGE AND HANDLING[13]

Q1: A supplier's written procedures should describe the proper handling of the inspection, measuring, and test instruments (including MSs) that were delivered from an outside source.

a. True

b. False

A: *True*

R: *Procedures should be provided to ensure that customer-supplied instruments are examined upon receipt for corrosion or physical damage. Instruments found to be unserviceable for use are recorded and reported to the customer. Instruments received in good condition should be handled and stored the same as company-owned instruments.*
Ref: Chapter 6, p. 120

Q2: MSs and M&TE shall be carefully handled during movement and use.

a. True

b. False

A: *True*

R: *M&TE shall be placed in containers or wrapped in moisture-free barrier materials and placed in suitable bins to ensure that the equipment maintains the required level of accuracy. Each measuring surface shall be cleaned with a lint-free cloth prior to use. Surfaces requiring protection against rust shall be coated with a film of corrosion-resistant oil when not in use.*
Ref: Chapter 2, p. 42 and chapter 6, p. 119

Q3:   Measurement standards do not have to be handled in the same way as inspection, measuring, and test equipment.

   a.   True

   b.   False

A: *False*

R: *All instruments should be stored, handled, and transported in such a manner as to protect them from damage, deterioration, and wear.*
Ref: Chapter 6, p. 119

N. TRACEABILITY[14]

Q1:   Certificates or reports from other than NIST or an independent laboratory shall attest to the fact that standards used in obtaining the calibration results have been compared with NIST or an international standard either directly or indirectly:

   a.   At the time of calibration or shortly thereafter

   b.   At planned intervals

   c.   Twice a year

A: *At the time of calibration or shortly thereafter*

R: *Feedback data are reviewed and analyzed by the metrology manager or a designated representative at the time of calibration or shortly thereafter to determine:*

   • *The adequacy of established calibration intervals*

   • *Whether there is a need to adjust calibration intervals*

- *Whether there is a need to modify established calibration procedures*

- *The adequacy of the calibration system and equipment reliability*

- *The identification of any out-of-tolerance equipment so that the equipment's use can be prevented until the reported deficiency has been corrected*

Ref: Chapter 2, p. 40

Q2: Normally, direct traceability to NIST standards is not required.

   a. True

   b. False

A: *True*

R: *One of the fundamental requirements of a calibration system is to ensure traceability of M&TE and MSs via an unbroken chain of calibrations to NIST or an international standard. Since most organizations do not do business directly with NIST or an international standard, the focus is centered on the independent laboratory that calibrates company standards.*
Ref: Chapter 6, p. 120

Q3: The ability to relate individual measurements to NIST through an unbroken chain of comparisons is known as:

   a. Calibration

   b. Traceability

   c. Accuracy conformance

   d. Verification

A: *Traceability*

R: *Traceability is the ability to trace the history, application, or location of an entity by means of recorded identification.*
Ref: Glossary, p. 203

Q4: Individual measurement results may be linked by an unbroken chain of comparisons via:

   a. A national standard

   b. An international standard

c. An independent calibration laboratory

d. A supplier's calibration laboratory

A: *An independent calibration laboratory, a supplier's calibration laboratory*

R: *Primary and secondary standards are traceable by an unbroken chain of calibration events to a national or international standard by the organization responsible for performing the calibration. Ref: Chapter 6, p. 106*

Q5: Besides NIST and an international standard, who else is authorized to perform higher-level standards calibration?

a. Capable independent calibration laboratories

b. Producers of products and services

c. Subcontractors

d. All of the above

A: *Capable independent calibration laboratories, producers of products and services*

R: *Independent calibration laboratories, as well as producers of products and services, can elect to perform higher-level calibrations with company-owned primary standards with a verified accuracy that is 10:1 or greater than their calibrated secondary standards. Ref: Chapter 6, p. 106*

O. CUMULATIVE EFFECT OF UNCERTAINTIES[15]

Q1: When evaluating the adequacy of calibration procedures, it is possible that several standards may be needed to perform a given calibration. One such procedure shows that three standards will be used together and have accuracies of 0.01 percent, 0.20 percent, and 0.04 percent. The combined error of the standards is 0.25 percent.

a. True

b. False

A: *True*

R: *Calibration procedures address the cumulative effect that the area of uncertainty has on products and services. The cumulative effect of the uncertainties includes each stage of the chain of calibrations, from primary standards to secondary standards to working M&TE.*
Ref: Chapter 6, p. 107

Q2: A calibration system description can include deviations from established uncertainty requirements.

    a. True

    b. False

A: *True*

R: *A calibration system description can include deviations only when state-of-the-art limitations preclude the use of accuracy ratios greater than 1:1.*
Ref: Chapter 2, p. 32

Q3: Documentation is not necessary when the collective area of uncertainty exceeds that percentage specified in an established quality plan.

    a. True

    b. False

A: *False*

R: *Documentation is an important function of the process. Without it, the selection of required MS and M&TE may be compromised.*
Ref: Chapter 1, p. 15

Q4: Calibration procedures do not have to address the cumulative effect an instrument's area of uncertainty has on products and services produced for customers.

    a. True

    b. False

A: *False*

R: *The cumulative effect of the uncertainties regarding each stage of calibrations—from primary through secondary standards to working M&TE to the product tolerance—shall be maintained. Ref: Chapter 6, p. 107*

P. ENVIRONMENTAL CONTROLS[16]

Q1: When ISO 10012-1:1992 is specified in a contract, temperature controls required for calibration of measuring instruments should be:

   a. 68 +/– 2° F, 35% +/– 5% relative humidity (RH)

   b. 72 +/– 1° F, 20–30% RH

   c. 68 +/– 2° F, 35–55% RH

   d. Controlled to the extent necessary

A: *Controlled to the extent necessary*

R: *Obtaining the accuracy of inspection, measuring, and test instruments within a controlled environment is accomplished to the extent necessary in order to maintain detrimental conditions within acceptable limits of the calibration being performed. Ref: Chapter 6, p. 121*

Q2: All environmental factors affecting the results of measurements must be considered when addressing environment factors.

   a. True

   b. False

A: *True*

R: *Environment elements that affect instrument accuracy include, temperature, humidity, dust (particle count), electrical and radio-frequency noise, and lighting. Ref: Chapter 2, p. 122*

Q3: Establishing environmental controls eliminates potential detrimental conditions that might affect the accuracy and stability of M&TE and MSs

   a. True

   b. False

A: *True*

R: *The extent of environmental controls include:*

- *The accuracy requirements of MSs*

- *The accuracy of M&TE*

- *The product tolerance*

Ref: Chapter 2, p. 121

Q4: Compensating corrections must be applied to calibration results in a *nonstandard* environment.

    a. True

    b. False

A: *True*

R: *Compensating corrections are made when appropriate. Ref: Chapter 6, p. 121*

Q5: Relevant environmental corrections shall be documented.

    a. True

    b. False

A: *True*

R: *Documentation is an important function of the calibration process. Without it, the selection of required MS and M&TE might be compromised. Timely documentation, when coordinated with inspection and testing requirements, will preclude the inadvertent omission of a contract quality requirement. Ref: Chapter 1, p. 14*

Q. PERSONNEL[17]

Q1: To ensure that measurements are made with the intended accuracy and ensure that all confirmations are properly performed, an organization's staff of managers should have certain characteristics and management support. What are they?

    a. Appropriate qualifications

    b. Training

    c. Experience

    d. Aptitude

    e. Supervision

    f. All of the above

A: *All of the above*

R: *Functions of calibration systems management are assigned to personnel who have achieved certification status from an accredited third party.*
Ref: Chapter 6, p. 122

Q2: Who is responsible for ensuring that qualified personnel are on hand to administer the metrology program?

    a. Client

    b. Supplier

    c. Subcontractor

    d. Independent calibration laboratory

    e. All of the above

A: *Supplier, subcontractor, independent calibration laboratory*

R: *The supplier and its subcontractors must ensure that qualified personnel are on hand to administer a metrology system.*
Ref: Chapter 7, p. 133

Q3: Who is responsible for identifying training needs that are associated with the application of a metrology program?

    a. Customer

    b. Supplier

    c. Subcontractor

A: *Suppliers, subcontractor*

R: *The suppliers of products and services identify the training needs of its metrology personnel and provide them with timely training.*
Ref: Chapter 7, p. 133

ENDNOTES

1. ISO 10012:2003, *Measurement management systems—Requirements for measurement processes and measuring equipment*, clause 6.3.1.
2. Ibid., clause 7.1.
3. Ibid., clause 8.2.
4. Ibid., clause 8.1.
5. Ibid., clause 7.3.
6. Ibid., clause 6.2.1.
7. Ibid., clause 6.2.3.
8. Ibid., clause 8.3.1.
9. Ibid., clause 7.1.
10. Ibid., clause 7.1.2.
11. Ibid., clause 7.1.3.
12. Ibid., clause 6.4.
13. Ibid., clause 8.3.3.
14. Ibid., clause 7.3.2.
15. Ibid., clause 7.3.1.
16. Ibid., clause 6.3.2.
17. Ibid., clause 6.1.

Glossary

accuracy—The closeness of agreement between an observed value and an accepted reference value.[1]

auditee—The organization being audited.[2]

calibration—The set of operations that establish, under specified conditions, the relationship between values indicated by a measuring instrument or measuring system, or values represented by a material measure or a reference material, and the corresponding values of a quantity realized by a reference standard.[3]

characteristic—A property that helps to differentiate between items of a given sample population. *Note:* The differentiation may be either quantitative (by variables) or qualitative (by attributes).[1]

comparator—An instrument for comparing some measurement with a fixed standard.[5]

competence—Documented ability to apply knowledge and skills.[6]

conformity—Fulfillment of specified requirements.[2]

contract review—Systematic activities carried out by the supplier before signing the contract to ensure that requirements for quality are adequately defined, free from ambiguity, documented, and can be realized by the supplier.[2]

contractor—Supplier in a contractual situation.[2]

corrective action—Action taken to eliminate the causes of an existing nonconformity, defect, or other undesirable situation in order to prevent recurrence.[2]

customer—Recipient of a product provided by the supplier.[2]

defect—Nonfulfillment of an intended usage requirement of reasonable expectation, including one concerned with safety.[2]

degree of documentation—Extent to which evidence is produced to provide confidence that specified requirements are fulfilled.[2]

disposition of nonconformity—Action to be taken to deal with an existing nonconforming entity in order to resolve the nonconformity.[2]

element—A quality of product, material, or service forming a cohesive entity on which a measurement or observation may be made.[1]

error of measurement—The result of a measurement minus the value of the measurand.[3]

hold point—Point defined in an appropriate document, beyond which an activity must not proceed without the approval of a designated organization or authority.[2]

inspection—The process of measuring, examining, testing, gaging, or otherwise comparing the unit with the applicable requirements.[1]

inspection by attributes—Inspection by attributes is inspection whereby either the unit of product is classified as conforming or nonconforming, or the number of nonconformities in the product is counted, with respect to a given requirement or a set of requirements.[4]

international standard—A standard, recognized by an international agreement, that serves as the basis for fixing the value of all other standards to the quality concerned.[3]

item—An object or quantity of material on which a set of observations can be made, or the result of making an observation of an object or quantity of material.[1]

limits of permissible error (of a measuring instrument)—The extreme values of an error permitted by specification, regulations, and so on, for a given measurement.[3]

management review—Formal evaluation by top management of the status and adequacy of the quality system in relation to quality policy and objectives.[2]

measurement control system—Set of interrelated or interacting elements necessary to achieve metrological confirmation and continued control of measurement processes.[6]

measurement process—Set of operations to determine the value of a quantity.[6]

measurement standards (MS)—A material measure, measuring instrument, reference material, or system intended to define, conserve, or reproduce a unit or one or more values of a quantity in order to transmit them to other measuring instruments by comparison.[3]

measuring equipment—All of the measuring instruments, measurement standards, reference materials, auxiliary apparatus, and instructions that are necessary to carry out a measurement. This includes measuring equipment used in calibrations.[3]

metrological characteristic—Distinguishing feature that can influence the results of a measurement.[6]

metrological confirmation—Set of operations required to ensure that a measuring instrument is in a state of compliance with the intended requirements.[3]

metrology—The science of measurements.[5]

metrology function—The function that has the responsibility for defining and implementing the measurement control system.[6]

model for quality assurance—Standardized or selected set of quality system requirements.[2]

national standard—A standard, recognized by a national agreement, that serves as the basis for fixing the value of all other standards to the quality concerned.[3]

nonconformity—Nonfulfillment of a specified requirement.[2]

objective evidence—Information that can be proved true, based on facts obtained through observation, measurement, test, or other means.[2]

organization—Company, corporation, firm, enterprise or institution, or a part thereof, whether incorporated or not, public or private, that has its own functions and administration.[2]

organizational structure—Responsibilities, authorities, and relationships, arranged in a pattern, through which an organization performs its functions.[2]

precision—The closeness of agreement between randomly selected individual measurements or test results.[1]

preventive action—Action taken to eliminate the causes of a potential nonconformity, defect, or other undesirable situation in order to prevent recurrence.[2]

purchaser—Customer in a contractual situation.[2]

qualification process—Process of demonstrating whether an entity is capable of fulfilling specified requirements.[2]

qualified—Status given to an entity when capability of fulfilling specified requirements has been demonstrated.[2]

quality—The totality of features and characteristics of a product or service that bears on its ability to satisfy given needs.[1]

quality assurance (QA)—All those planned or systematic actions necessary to provide adequate confidence that a product or service will satisfy given needs.[1]

quality audit—A systematic and independent examination to determine whether quality activities and related results comply with planned arrangements and whether these arrangements are implemented effectively and are suitable to achieve objectives.[3]

quality audit observation—Statement of fact during a quality audit and substantiated by objective evidence.[2]

quality auditor—Person qualified to perform quality audits.[2]

quality control (QC)—The operational techniques and the activities that sustain a quality of product or service that will satisfy given needs; also the use of such techniques and activities.[1]

quality evaluation—Systematic examination of the extent to which an entity is capable of fulfilling specified requirements.[2]

quality losses—Losses caused by not realizing the potential of resources in processes and activities.[2]

quality management—The totality of functions involved in the determination and achievement of quality.[1]

quality manual—Document stating the quality policy and describing the quality system of an organization.[2]

quality plan—Document setting out the specific quality practices, resources, and sequence of activities relevant to a particular product, project, or contract.[2]

quality policy—Overall intentions and direction of an organization with regard to quality, as formally expressed by top management.[2]

quality-related costs—Those costs incurred in ensuring satisfactory quality, as well as the losses incurred when satisfactory quality is not achieved.[2]

quality surveillance—Continued monitoring and verification of the status of an entity and analysis of records to ensure that specification requirements are being fulfilled.[2]

quality system—Organizational structure, procedures, processes, and resources needed to implement quality management.[2]

reference conditions—Conditions of use for a measuring instrument prescribed for performance testing or to ensure intercomparison of results of measurements.[3]

reference material—A material or substance, one or more properties of which are sufficiently well established to be used for the calibration of an apparatus, the assessment of a measurement method, or the assignment of values to materials.[3]

requirement for quality—Expression of the needs or their translation into a set of quantitatively or quantitatively stated requirements for the characteristics of an entity to enable its realization and examination.[2]

specification—Document stating requirements.[2]

subcontractor—Organization that provides a product to the supplier.[2]

supplier—Organization that provides a product to a customer.[2]

testing—A means of determining the capability of an item to meet specified requirements by subjecting the item to a set of physical, chemical, environmental, or operation actions and conditions.[1]

traceability—Ability to trace the history, application, or location of an entity by means of recorded identification.[2]

total quality management (TQM)—Management approach of an organization that is centered on quality, based on the participation of its members, aimed at long-term success through customer satisfaction, and beneficial to all members of the organization and to society.[2]

uncertainty—An indication of the variability associated with a measured value that takes into account two major components of error: (1) bias and (2) the random error attributed to the impression of the measurement process.[1]

unit—A quantity of product, material, or service forming a cohesive entity on which a measurement or observation may be made.[1]

variables, method of—Measurement of quality by measuring and recording the numerical magnitude of a quality characteristic for each of the units in the group under consideration. This involves reference to a continuous scale of some kind.[1]

verification—Confirmation by examination and provision of objective evidence that specified requirements have been filled.[2]

SOURCES FOR GLOSSARY TERMS

1. ASQ Statistics Division, *Glossary and Tables for Statistical Quality Control*, 3d ed. (Milwaukee: ASQC Quality Press, 1996).
2. ANSI/ISO/ASQC A8402-1994, *Quality Management and Quality Assurance—Vocabulary.*
3. ISO 10012-1:1992, *Quality Assurance Requirements for Measuring Equipment—Part 1: Metrological Confirmation System for Measuring Equipment.*
4. ANSI/ASQC Z1.4-1998, *Sampling Procedures and Tables for Inspection by Attributes.*
5. *Webster's New World Dictionary of the American Language* (Springfield, MA: G&C Merriam Co., 1975).
6. ANSI/ISO/ASQ Q9000-2000, *Quality Management Systems—Fundamentals and Vocabulary.*

Acronyms

ANSI	American National Standards Institute
ASQ	American Society for Quality
CEO	Chief executive officer
CI	Calibration interval
CP	Calibration procedure
FOB	Free on board
GIDEP	Government and Industry Data Exchange Program
HRT	Hourly rate of technician
IEC	International Electrotechnical Commission
ISO	International Organization for Standardization
M&TAT	Measuring and test equipment accuracy tolerance
M&TE	Measuring and test equipment
MRB	Material review board
MS	Measurement standard
NCSL	National Conference of Standards Laboratories
NIST	National Institute of Standards and Technology

NLI	Number of like items
PAT	Primary standard accuracy tolerance
PR	Preliminary review
PSIG	Pounds per square inch gage
QA	Quality assurance
QC	Quality control
R	Ratio
R&R	Repeatability and reproducibility
SAT	Secondary standard accuracy tolerance
TQM	Total quality management

Bibliography

ANSI/ASQC M1-1996. *American National Standard for Calibration Systems.*

ANSI/ASQC Z1.4-1998. *Sampling Procedures and Tables for Inspection by Attributes.*

ANSI/ISO 17025-1999. *General Requirements for the Competence of Testing and Calibration Laboratories.*

ANSI/ISO/ASQ Q9000-2000. *Quality Management Standards–Fundamentals and Vocabulary.*

ANSI/ISO/ASQ Q9001-2000. *Quality Management Standards–Requirements.*

ANSI/ISO/ASQ Q9004-2000. *Quality Management Standards–Guidelines for Performance Improvements.*

ANSI/ISO/ASQC A8402-1994. *Quality Management and Quality Assurance–Vocabulary.*

ANSI/ISO/ASQC Q10011-1994. *Guidelines for Auditing Quality Systems.*

ANSI/NCSL Z540-1-1994. *Calibration Laboratories and Measuring and Test Equipment—General Requirements.*

ASQ Statistics Division. *Glossary and Tables for Statistical Quality Control,* 3rd ed. Milwaukee: ASQC Quality Press, 1996.

Campanella, Jack. *Principles of Quality Costs: Principles, Implementation, and Use,* 3rd ed. Milwaukee: ASQ Quality Press, 1999.

Chrysler/Ford/General Motors Supply Quality Requirements Task Force. QS-9000. *Quality System Requirements.* 1995.

Griffith, Gary. *Quality Technician's Handbook.* Upper Saddle River, NJ: Prentice Hall, 2003.

ISO 10012-1:1992. *Quality Assurance Requirements for Measuring Equipment— Part 1: Metrological Confirmation System for Measuring Equipment.*

ISO 10012-2003. *Measurement management systems—Requirements for measurement processes and measuring equipment.*

ISO 13485:2003. *Quality Management Systems—Medical Devices—System Requirements For Regulatory Purposes.*

U.S. Department of Defense. MIL-STD-120. *Gage Inspection.* 1963.

U.S. Department of Defense. MIL-STD-45662A. *Calibration System Requirements.* 1988.

U.S. Department of Defense, General Services Administration, and National Aeronautics and Space Administration. *Federal Acquisition Regulation.* 1995.

U.S. Department of Defense and National Aeronautics and Space Administration. *DoD/NASA-HDBK Q9000.* 1994.

Wortman, Bill. *CQE Primer: The Quality Engineer Primer,* 6th ed. West Terre Haute, IN: Quality Council of Indiana, 2000.

Index